JUDO ON THE GROUND

KESAGATAME OR SCARF HOLD demonstrated by G. Whyman, 2nd Dan against D. Bloss, 2nd Dan

JUDO ON THE GROUND

The Oda (9th Dan) Method

"KATAMEWAZA"

An Interpretation of the
Oda System comprising
numerous drastic Immobilizations,
Necklocks and Dislocation
Methods hitherto unknown
in the West

BY

E. J. HARRISON

(3Rd Dan)

Line drawings by JAK
Photographs by I. MORRIS

Originally published 1959

To my dearest friend, MALCOLM J. GREGORY, 4th Dan of the TOKYO KEISHICHO TAIIKUKAN (Tokyo Metropolitan Police Dojo), a great English Yudansha, the first foreigner and only non-policeman ever to have been awarded a Yodan certificate by that Dojo, I dedicate this book as an inadequate token of gratitude for his invaluable co-operation without which it could not have been compiled.

CONTENTS

FOREWORD

IT affords me much pleasure to place on record my gratitude to "Jak" for his excellent line-drawings which greatly facilitate the task of understanding the printed explanations of the corresponding techniques. As intimated on the title-page the information contained in these pages is based on the original text of Tsunetani Oda's work dealing with Judo on the Ground, otherwise Katamewaza. Thanks alike to "Jak's" artistic talent and personal knowledge of Judo he has been able to impart to these drawings a clarity too often lacking in the photographs and line-drawings which are generally used to elucidate the latest locks and holds in the art of Judo.

The special photographs of certain selected methods of Katamewaza have been taken at The Budokwai by J. Morris 2nd Dan. These methods are ably demonstrated by leading Yudansha of The Budokwai in the persons of D. Bloss 2nd Dan, G. Whyman 2nd Dan, R. Bowen 1st Dan and A. Bain 1st Dan. I tender my thanks to one and all for their valuable co-operation.

When engaged in the congenial task of applying the Oda system of Katamewaza on the mat I feel sure that all Judoka will derive satisfaction from the exercise of individual ingenuity and resourcefulness in devising effective Kaeshiwaza pertinent to the more unorthodox "te" taken from the Oda repertoire. And I further venture to express the hope that my rendering of Oda's skilled exposition of this particular branch, now published for the first time in this country, will add considerably to the knowledge of those that study and practise the art of Judo.

Lastly, I do not presume so far as to say that this book is wholly free from errors. Indeed it is safe to assert that no such work on this difficult and complicated subject has yet appeared in any language. However, I trust that these are not likely to detract from the value of the book as a whole in this particular domain.

E. J. H.

19 Mornington Avenue,
London, W. 14.

CHAPTER I
INTRODUCTORY REMARKS

THE present volume is in no sense designed as a manual for beginners. On the contrary, it presupposes on the part of the reader some prior practical and theoretical knowledge of the art of Judo and reasonable familiarity with its Japanese and English terminology. The scope of the book is confined to an exposition and a clarification of the second overall division of Judo known as Katamewaza which in turn comprises three sub-divisions styled respectively (1) Osaekomiwaza or Immobilization Holds, more briefly "hold-downs"; (2) Shimewaza or Shiboriwaza otherwise Necklocks, and (3) Kansetsuwaza or Dislocation Locks or Holds. A popular synonym for all three sub-divisions of Katamewaza is Newaza for which the current English equivalent is "Groundwork".

Although perhaps, in view of what I have already said, the caution is superfluous, I must emphasize that unless the reader is already fairly proficient in Nagewaza or throwing methods, he should not lightly undertake the task of specializing in Newaza, because while admittedly Newaza as such differ appreciably from Nagewaza in the demands they impose upon the Judoka's muscular system, yet since in some instances the initial attack to create an opening for recourse to Newaza is made from the standing position, an assailant comparatively ignorant of Tachiwaza or standing techniques and bent upon applying Newaza would at the very outset be at a grave disadvantage if opposed to an adversary well versed in that branch of the art. He might indeed be thrown before he could reach the stage of Kuzushi let alone Tsukuri and Kake!

For the information contained in these pages I disclaim all credit in advance, apart from the labour involved in my arduous but voluntary role of interpreter of sage counsel emanating from a famous Japanese Shihan or instructor named Tsunetani Oda, 9th Dan of the Tokyo Kodokan, admittedly the greatest living authority on Newaza. This information has been culled from his popular work in Japanese entitled Judo wa ko shite susume ("Progress by doing Judo this way"). However, the present volume is in no sense a literal translation of Oda's book which covers Judo as a whole; my special concern has been to do justice to the section in the original dealing with Newaza and this not by slavishly adhering to the Japanese author's

1

handling of the theme but rather by the eclectic method which justifies the exercise of discretion and the rejection of material which, in my opinion, is of minor value or extraneous to the general purpose I have in view. Nor is it any reflection upon the distinguished author to say that some of his methods impress me as far-fetched and as such likely to fail when attempted against a normally alert opponent of one's own Judo grading. Nevertheless the ample residue should suffice to afford a rich mine of Newaza knowledge upon which the aspirant can usefully draw to help him in his training under this particular head.

As the reader will notice, in my attempted interpretation of what may be called the Oda system of Newaza I have adhered to the orthodox sequence observed in all reliable books on Judo, viz. Osaekomiwaza, Shimewaza and Kansetsuwaza in that order.

I do not think that a laboured disquisition on the respective and comparative merits of Newaza and Nagewaza would serve any useful purpose. It may well be said that the two branches of the art are inter-complementary, and that for the fashioning of the complete Judoka mastery of both is indispensable. Doubtless we have here a counsel of perfection by no means easy of practical assimilation. What is sometimes loosely called the personal equation cannot be wholly excluded, and I must admit that during my own long association with Japanese Yudansha at the Tokyo Kodokan and elsewhere I rarely met anybody immune from individual preference not only for one or other of the several branches and sub-divisions of the art but even for some particular "te" or trick in which he was everywhere known to excel. How otherwise could it happen that we have in Judo parlance the word "Tokuiwaza" meaning in the vernacular "pet throw"?

It may be adduced in criticism of Osaekomiwaza more especially that as compared with Nagewaza they are not so spectacular and that as an expedient for "knocking out" an opponent for the count their repertoire is much less effective than that of Nagewaza. Superficially considered this criticism seems plausible. But if we take the trouble to examine the issues more closely we shall see that Osaekomiwaza cannot logically be divorced from the other two sub-divisions of Katamewaza, viz. Shimewaza or Necklocks and Kansetsuwaza or Dislocation Locks, and that as applied by a skilled Yudansha of the Oda calibre an Osaekomiwaza or Immobilization Hold may as often as not be converted into a more drastic and painful lock from the other two sub-divisions with such lightning speed as to entitle the transition to be regarded as almost a reflex action executed in quasi-intuitive or involuntary response to hostile stimulus. And although the Osaekomi methods are fraught with less danger to the victim's body and for that reason may be safely practised by Judoka until a much more advanced age than Nagewaza, all three branches of Katamewaza afford an ideal means for the cultivation not only of great physical endurance, bodily and mental alertness in swift adaptation to an ever-changing situation, but also the moral qualities of perseverance, steadfastness of purpose, concentration, cool judgment and presence of mind to cope with an emergency. Nor is the criticism sometimes voiced of Osaekomi methods that they are less efficacious than Nagewaza for the annihilation of an opponent in a real life and death struggle applicable to Shimewaza and Kansetsuwaza. Indeed, without in any way seeking to underrate a good Judo throw as a means of discouraging a too importunate thug or cosh boy, yet in a fight *an outrance* and should you deem it necessary to administer the quietus to your assailant not "with a bare bodkin" but with your bare hands, then we must surely concede that a necklock or dislocation hold from the prolific and protean Katamewaza otherwise Newaza repertoire would prove more decisive.

Another point in favour of Newaza is that to a greater extent perhaps than Nagewaza they tend to encourage the *offensive* spirit among their votaries for the attainment of victory. That is not to question the validity of the same principle in Nagewaza, but in the latter branch there is sometimes discernible among Judoka an inclination to act more upon the *defensive* to avoid being thrown, so that the human phenomenon of the Judoka classified in Japanese as *tori-nikui* (literally, "difficult to take") is by no means uncommon in every Judo Dojo. Owing maybe to the less disconcerting effect of a hold-down than a heavy throw, young and old Judoka can more successfully withstand this temptation and be brought to realize that persistence in attack will be the shortest cut to victory. And irrespective of these considerations it cannot be gainsaid that for the development of the finest type of Judo physique Newaza are an indispensable corollary to Nagewaza.

Elsewhere in the following pages I have pointed out that most of the relevant methods are described as applied from your opponent's right side in conformity with the general rule observed in such cases and on the justifiable assumption that any intelligent Judoka, having mastered the right side or right hand approach, should experience no difficulty in making the essential readjustments for a left side or left hand approach. It must indeed be emphasized that the complete Judoka ought properly to be ambidextrous and able to use either arm, as also either leg, with equal facility.

I may hardly dare to hope that this little book is free from mistakes. Indeed my "will hath in it a more modest working", to paraphrase a successful exponent of another cruder style of mat-work. In mitigation of such inevitable laches I would plead that I err in good company because I feel sure that the vast sports bibliography generally and the Judo branch thereof particularly have not yet given birth to a *magnum opus* justified in repudiating "the soft impeachment".

CHAPTER II
GENERAL SURVEY OF OSAEKOMIWAZA

ASSUMING that you are the assailant in Osaekomiwaza, then your specific aim can be summarized as to pin your opponent to the ground or mat and in this way control his freedom of movement and prevent him in contest from rising for thirty seconds. And for the achievement of this purpose it is essential that (1) your opponent should be lying on his back, and (2) that you yourself should be uppermost from whatever direction or angle you may be attacking so as to dominate your opponent's freedom of action. On the other hand, if you begin your attack from a standing position then you should be sure that you retain the initiative and cannot be thrown before you have succeeded in bringing your opponent down on the mat either supine, on his stomach, on his knees, half sitting, or on all-fours to facilitate the breakdown of his defences and your effective entry for the application of the appropriate immobilization method. And from first to last you must try to guard against a position in which your opponent has contrived to entwine your torso with his legs or to hook or entangle your legs with his.

Although as in every other branch of Judo the importance of strength is frankly recognized by all the leading Japanese authorities, its misuse and reckless dissipation will from the very nature of the struggle more surely exhaust the tyro when engaged in Newaza than in Nagewaza. This contention is especially true of the Osaekomiwaza we are now considering. Since your purpose is to prevent your supine opponent from getting up while his purpose is to get up or to apply a counter, you must ever be on the alert to concentrate your strength against the direction from which he is trying to rise. As a general rule and for anatomical reasons the main danger points are the shoulders, helped of course by the violent oscillations of legs and torso, as your opponent strives *inter alia* to create a gap between your body and either flank of his own body as a precursor to counter measures or Kaeshiwaza. Do not therefore fritter away your energies upon points of non-resistance but keep a surplus of strength in reserve for the moment when it is urgently needed to foil your opponent's serious efforts to shake you off or, as mentioned earlier, to hold your torso between his legs or to hook or entangle your legs with his. As regards quiescent parts, exemplify rather the rationale of Judo by relaxing your exertions and keeping your body soft, pliant, supple and untensed yet ever ready at a moment's notice to bear heavily down upon the spot or area from which danger threatens. Inductive proof of the amazing degree to which this sort of sixth sense can be cultivated so as to offset the disadvantages of a by no means robust physique was afforded during my active membership of the old Kodokan by a Yudansha whose weight when stripped could not have exceeded ten stone but whose skill in Newaza was so uncanny that time and time again in both Randori and Shiai he defeated opponents of twelve, thirteen or more stone with his immobilization holds, whereas in Tachiwaza many a Mudansha, myself included, could throw him easily. And the secret of his success consisted precisely in his ability to conserve his energies, to shift his body with lightning speed in automatic or reflex response to his undermost opponent's every move and in this manner to wear down his opponent until the fatal thirty seconds had expired.

Those of my readers that have studied my *Manual of Judo* do not need to be told that one other attribute conducive to success in Newaza as in Nagewaza is a well-developed saika tanden or lower abdomen in the absence of which the open sesame to distinction in the art is likely to be denied the aspirants. And for an explanation of the manner in which you can effect that development by means of deep abdominal breathing or *fukushiki kokyu* I must refer you to that manual.

In his treatment of Osaekomiwaza Oda describes first the immobilization methods themselves (Osaekata), then the variations, changes or mutations (Henka) involved, and finally the many methods of breaking through your opponent's defences and so effecting an entry (Hairikata), and although perhaps a more logical sequence would seem to relegate the Osaekata to the last place, I shall follow his example, leaving it to my readers to study the actual techniques in the light of his Henka and Hairikata.

He divides the Osaekomiwaza into three main categories or systems designated as follows: (1) Kesagatame-kei or Scarf Hold system, (2) Shihogatame-kei or Locking of the Four Quarters system, and (3) Ukegatame-kei or Floating Lock system.

In the Kesagatame-kei you keep the upper part of your body upright, your torso held obliquely in close contact with your opponent. In the Shihogatame-kei you are more or less lying on your stomach or on all-fours but in such wise as to maintain contact between your own and your opponent's chest and abdomen. In the Ukegatame-kei you are attacking your opponent in a half-sitting, half-rising posture.

For the Kesagatame-kei there are four basic approaches as follows:

Scarf (Kesa) A: As you lie on your right side on the mat your right leg is stretched out, its outer side held in contact with the mat. Your left leg is drawn up behind with the inside knee held against the mat. Both legs are spread to an extent that will not impair their elasticity. Your right side is supported with your right arm held against the mat with the elbow bent (Fig. A-1).

Fig. A-1

Scarf B: Your right leg is thrust forward in much the same way as in Scarf A, with the outer side against the mat. Your left leg is more widely separated from your right leg and sharply bent at the knee with the entire sole planted on the mat (Fig. B-1).

Fig. B-1

Scarf C: Again your right leg is stretched out to the front with its outer edge against the mat. Your left knee is bent and the inner side of the big toe pressed against the mat. In this case, however, the space between your legs is much reduced (Fig. C-1).

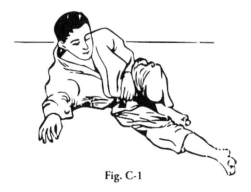

Fig. C-1

Scarf D: The outer edge of your right leg touches the mat with the knee bent. Your left leg is thrust to the front overlapping your right leg, with the ball of the foot held against the mat (Fig. D-1).

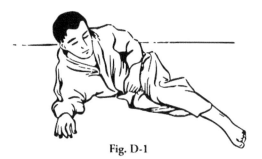

Fig. D-1

Next we have the Shihogatame-kei in which seven ways of holding the legs are exemplified as follows:

A: You squat on both legs with the upper part of your body bent forward and your elbows and forearms resting on the mat (Fig. A-2).

Fig. A-2

B: In this stance you are seated in such a way that one or other of your legs is disposed so that the part below the knee juts out to the side. In the attached Fig, B-2 the left leg is in that position.

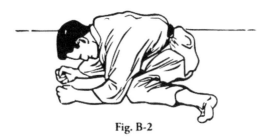

Fig. B-2

C: You squat on your right leg while your left leg is stretched out to the side with either the entire sole of the foot or its inner side held against the mat (Fig. C-2).

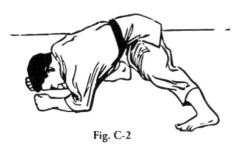

Fig. C-2

D: Both legs are outstretched with thighs opened and held against the mat (Fig. D-2).

Fig. D-2

E: Both thighs are opened and held against the mat and the right leg is bent to the inside (Fig. E).

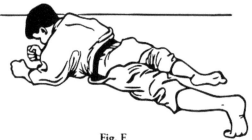

Fig. E

F: Both legs are spread, your hips are raised, the tips of your toes against the mat and your head lowered (Fig. F).

Fig. F

G: You are lying on your stomach, both legs opened with the feet touching each other (Fig. G).

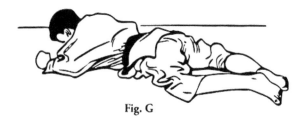

Fig. G

The foregoing seven approaches demonstrate *inter alia* the complete squatting posture and one with the hips raised and the tips of the toes held against the mat.

However, it is pointed out that Henka or possible variations are so numerous that it would not be possible to enumerate them all in detail. When therefore you are actually tackling an opponent on the mat you must ever be watchful to counter all his movements and to seize the right moment for exerting maximum strength in the necessary direction in order to effect an entry. By knowing almost instinctively when you should switch from a Shihogatame-kei to a Kesagatame-kei or vice versa, always being prepared to coordinate these approaches and to supplement one with the other, you can most surely achieve your intended purpose.

CHAPTER III
EXPOSITION OF OSAEKOMIWAZA

THE first method on Oda's list is, in accordance with universal usage, the HONGESAGATAME, otherwise the KESAGATAME or Fundamental Scarf Hold. It is described as follows:

It is assumed that your opponent is already lying on his back and that you are attacking him from his right side. You should establish contact with your opponent's chest area obliquely from your right side chest to your abdominal region. Your right arm is passed from the tip of his left shoulder across the back of his neck.

With his right elbow-joint as centre you trap his right arm firmly in your left armpit so as to control his freedom of action. Your right leg is stretched to the front with its outer edge against the mat. Your right thigh is so disposed as to be in contact with your opponent's back neck or upper part of his back. Your left leg is conveniently stretched to your left with its inner edge touching the mat. Your head is raised together with the upper part of your body. Then as you press against your opponent with your right side chest you impart a bending action against him from his neck to the upper part of his torso and in this manner immobilize him (Fig. 1).

Fig. 1

13

POSITION OF HEAD:

Your forehead may be pressed against the mat. This movement can be effective when dealing with a comparatively tall opponent. If he tries to roll you over to his left side, it may suffice to advance your forehead only so far as his head in order to foil his efforts.

VARIANTS IN USE OF RIGHT ARM:

(1) This arm may be extended from its position round your opponent's neck to be placed in your right groin.

(2) Or you can grasp your trousers in the neighbourhood of your right groin.

(3) Or you can use your right hand so as to grip your opponent from his right side collar to his front collar, your thumb inside.

(4) Or the palm of your right hand may be placed on the mat near the tip of your opponent's left shoulder.

VARIANTS IN USE OF LEFT ARM:

(1) Your left arm may be wound round your opponent's right arm from the outside so that with your right hand you can grip his right front collar.

(2) Without pinning your opponent's right arm in your left armpit you may pass your left arm from the outside of his right arm and grip his right front collar.

(3) You may employ both arms to confine your opponent's neck.

POSITION OF LEFT LEG:

(1) The sole of your left foot may be entirely placed against the mat with the knee raised.

(2) The sole of your left foot may be placed against the mat with the knee raised as before, but assuming that you have not pinned your opponent's right arm in your left armpit you may press the inner side of the knee heavily against his right elbow-joint to help in preventing the withdrawal of his right arm.

POSITION OF THE BODY:

You may be on your stomach with your right knee bent under you, your left leg trailing obliquely to the rear.

KUZURE-KESAGATAME
(BROKEN SCARF HOLD)

Your opponent is as before lying on his back and you are attacking him from his right side. Your right waist is applied to his right front waist, close contact being established obliquely from your right side stomach to your armpit with his torso from his abdominal region to his left chest. Your right front waist is slightly protruded.

Your right hand threaded through his left armpit firmly grips his right side collar while your left hand pins his right wrist in your left armpit to prevent its withdrawal. Your right leg is opened out to the front to the fullest extent and brought into close contact with your opponent from kneecap to thigh passing from under his right flank between his right shoulder and back. The outside of your right foot touches the mat.

With your right thigh you impart a lifting feeling to your opponent's upper torso. Your left leg is stretched well to the rear with its inner side against the mat. It should be held in such a way as not to deprive it of freedom of variation (Henka) when necessary. Your head should be raised with your face turned to the front. In this manner you may be' able to immobilize your opponent (Fig. 2).

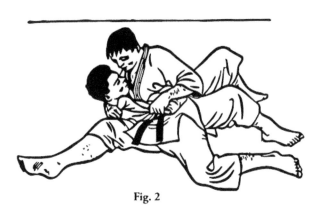

Fig. 2

POSITION OF THE HEAD:

Your face may be turned to your left, your right cheek held against your opponent's right cheek and your forehead almost touching the mat.

VARIANTS IN USE OF RIGHT ARM:

(1) Your right elbow may be pressed against your opponent's left side chest, the arm extended and the palm applied to the mat at his left upper side.

(2) Your right hand may grip your opponent's front collar from the direction of his left side collar so that your right wrist passes from over his left front chest under his (left) armpit and your right elbow rests on the mat.

(3) Your right hand palm is spread (on the mat) between your opponent's left arm and left flank.

METHOD OF HOLDING WITH LEFT HAND AND ACTION OF LEFT ARM:

(1) With your opponent's right elbow-joint as centre or pivot you control him.

(2) Your left arm and hand are wound round your opponent's right arm from the outside and hold it tightly. The upper part of your body is bent down so that your forehead is placed on the mat.

(3) Your left hand is passed from outside your opponent's right side arm to grip his back collar from the direction of his right front collar.

(4) Your left armpit immobilizes your opponent's right arm while your left arm is wound round that arm from the outside and passing underneath seizes his right front collar.

POSITION OF LEFT LEG:

This is the same as in the Hongesagatame.

POSITION OF BODY:

The same as in the Hongesagatame.

Kesagatame (effected with opponent's head under right armpit):

Attacking as before from your supine opponent's right side you trap his right arm under your left armpit. Then your right arm is passed across your opponent's back neck so that the forearm is thrust into his left front armpit. Your legs are disposed as in the normal Kesagatame. Your opponent's head and neck protrude from under your right back armpit and by means of forward bending pressure against his neck and torso you may control his freedom of movement (Fig. 3).

Fig. 3

Kuzure-Kesagatame (effected from opponent's head):

Your opponent has fallen on his back and you have moved round in the direction of his head on the right hand side. Now with your left hand passed over his left shoulder and back you contrive to grasp his back belt midway or his right back belt.

Your right hand is thrust into his left armpit. Your right leg is pushed from his right side neck in the direction of his left armpit so that his back neck rests on your right thigh and the outside of your leg is held in contact with the mat. Your left leg is extended to the rear in such wise that the inner side of the knee-cap presses the mat.

The upper part of your body is bent forward and in this way you may immobilize your opponent. In this case it is also permissible to grip your trousers at the right knee with your right hand (Fig. 4).

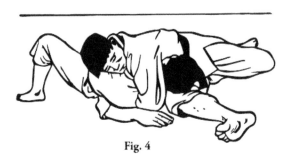

Fig. 4

Kuzure-Kesagatame (effected by enfolding opponent's neck with left arm):

Your opponent is on his back and you are attacking from his right side. You must establish contact obliquely from your side chest to your abdominal region with your opponent's chest and abdomen. Your right hand is passed over your opponent's left armpit to seize his left shoulder. The disposition of your hips and waist and the manner of using your legs are the same as in the Kuzure-Kesagatame. Your left arm passing from over your opponent's right neck and looped under it grasps his left front collar in the normal hold, i.e. palm downwards, fingers outside and thumb inside collar. His right arm is controlled with your right waist and thigh. As a rule you establish contact between your right side back waist and your opponent's right flank and apply pressure. But your body should not be stiffened but kept soft and pliant to immobilize your opponent (Fig. 5).

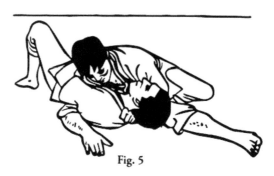

Fig. 5

VARIANTS IN USE OF RIGHT HAND:

(1) Your right hand may be linked with your opponent's left shoulder.

(2) Or your right hand may be planted on the mat at your opponent's left side.

POSITION OF LEGS:

(1) They may take the position of Fig. B-1, Fig. D-1, Fig. B-2, Fig. C-2 or Fig. E, according to circumstances.

(2) With your right leg in the squatting position you may thrust the right knee-cap against your opponent's chest. Your left leg may be bent to the inside, the outer edge held in contact with the mat.

(3) Your opponent's right arm may be clamped between both your legs.

MAKURA-KESAGATAME
(PILLOW-SCARF HOLD)

Your opponent is lying on his back and you have moved on the mat towards his head on his right. Your right waist is brought into close contact with the space between his right shoulder and neck. Your right leg is stretched to the front and your left leg to the rear with the inner knee surface against the mat. Exemplifying the term "pillow", your opponent's head, more precisely his back neck, rests upon your right thigh. Your right hand is passed over his left armpit and is laid with all the fingers spread evenly upon your right knee or else you grip your trousers with that hand. Your left hand grasps your opponent's back collar from the direction of his right side neck, your thumb inside. Imparting an upward tightening action so that your opponent cannot extricate his neck, you bend forward the upper part of your body and immobilize him (Fig. 6).

Fig. 6

USHIRO-KESAGATAME
(REAR SCARF HOLD)

Your opponent is lying on his back and for the application of this method you have moved to his left side near his head with your back turned towards it. You must establish contact obliquely between your two bodies from your own right waist to your side chest and abdomen and from your opponent's left shoulder to his chest. You pin your opponent's left wrist tightly in your left armpit, and with your right elbow press strongly against his upper arm. Your right front waist is somewhat protruded. Your right leg is extended to the front with its outer edge against the mat. Your left leg is stretched obliquely to the rear with the under surface of the knee-cap held against the mat. Be careful to retain freedom of Henka or change in the position of the leg. Your right side chest is pushed strongly against your opponent's neck and throat. The upper part of your body is twisted slightly to your left front. In this manner you may immobilize your opponent (Fig. 7).

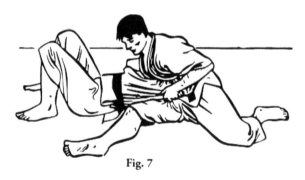

Fig. 7

VARIANTS IN USE OF RIGHT HAND:

(1) You may grip your opponent's right side belt with your right hand

(2) Or your right hand may be passed under his right back armpit to take hold of his right side belt.

VARIANTS IN USE OF LEFT HAND:

(1) Your left hand may pass over your opponent's left forearm and take hold of his left side belt or you may plant your spread palm on the mat or you may thrust your left hand under your opponent's body.

(2) With your left hand you may grip your opponent's trousers on the inside of his left knee-joint and manipulate it so as to cause his thighs to spread.

(3) You may insert your left hand from above both your opponent's thighs passing from over his right leg and grip his trousers at the buttocks or right side hip or grasp his right side belt.

(4) Your left hand may be passed from your opponent's left armpit to hold his left side belt or may be placed on the mat.

(5) Your left hand may be left entirely free to be used as occasion demands.

POSITION OF LEGS:
This may be according to Fig. D-1 described in Chapter II.

Ushiro-Kesagatame (effected by control of opponent's left arm with armpit):
It is assumed that your opponent has fallen not flat on his back but with his right shoulder tending to be a little more lowered to the side. You attack from the back of his head, your body facing to the left. Your left hand is passed under his left rear armpit to grasp your own left front collar so that his upper arm is firmly enfolded. When his forearm is bent you pin it in your right armpit. Simultaneously your right leg is stretched to the front as in the Kesagatame and your left leg extended to the rear as in the normal Ushiro-Kesagatame. The fingers of your right hand are hitched to the inner side of your right thigh from above. With the crushing pressure of your right armpit you apply gyaku to your opponent's left arm. Your left hand pulls strongly, the upper part of your body is turned to the left and in this way you immobilize your opponent (Fig. 8).

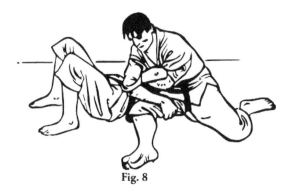

Fig. 8

KESAGATAME-KEI KATAGATAME
(SCARF HOLD SYSTEM SHOULDER LOCK)

Your opponent is on his back and you are attacking him from his right side. The adjustment of your hips and waist and the disposal of your legs are virtually the same as in the Hongesagatame. Your right hand and arm are passed over the tip of your opponent's left shoulder round his neck. Your left hand is thrust from under his right armpit to meet and clasp your right hand behind your opponent's neck. Your forehead is lowered to the mat. Your right chest is brought into contact with your opponent's right chest and as the result of these movements his right upper arm is, as it were, locked between your right side neck and your opponent's right side neck.

The rightward pressure of your right shoulder, which forces his right arm uncomfortably over to his left, coupled with the leftward traction of your joined hands behind his neck, effectively immobilizes him.

The best way of joining your hands is to cup, so to speak, your right hand in the palm of your left hand which is held upwards. And as Oda points out, if while drawing your joined hands leftward towards yourself you contrive to press the thumb edge of your right wrist strongly against your opponent's left carotid artery you can convert this Osaekomiwaza into a Shimewaza and perhaps extort your opponent's submission. The Japanese term for this combination method is Kenyoho (Fig. 9).

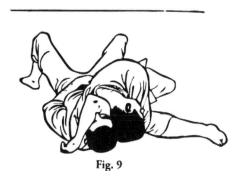

Fig. 9

SHIHOGATAME-KEI KATAGATAME
(LOCKING OF FOUR QUARTERS SYSTEM SHOULDER LOCK)

As before your opponent is on his back and you are attacking from his right side. In this case, however, your right knee is bent with your shin on the mat and as much as possible you adhere to your opponent from your right side chest to your back with a pushing sensation.

The upper part of your body is prostrate, your buttocks are somewhat raised. Your left leg is stretched obliquely to the left side with the sole of the foot against the mat.

Your joint hand hold is the same as in the Kesagatame-kei Katagatame already described. Your right front abdominal region touches your opponent's right front chest and you reinforce the pressure with the upper part of your body. And as in the case of the Kesagatame-kei Katagatame you can convert the hold into a necklock and so extort surrender. As a leg variant your right knee may be thrust against your opponent's right back (Fig. 10).

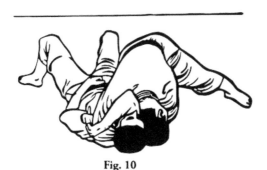

Fig. 10

KAMISHIHOGATAME
(UPPER LOCKING OF THE FOUR QUARTERS)

With your opponent lying on his back you attack him from behind his head.

Squatting on the mat you first sandwich his head between your thighs. Your right hand is passed under his right and your left hand under his left armpit to grasp his right and left side belt respectively. Your face may be turned optionally to either your right or left.

Close contact must be established between your chest and that of your opponent. Both your elbows should strongly constrict his torso from both sides. Try to concentrate as much weight and strength as possible in your buttocks.

It goes without saying that in the course of this hold-down you will be bound to change the initial position of your legs to counter your opponent's efforts to shake you off. Thus in accordance with the directions given in Chapter II you may find it necessary to stretch one or both legs behind to the fullest extent and to spread your thighs or to raise your hips with the tips of your toes against the mat.

There must be complete coordination between your torso and extremities so that from whatever direction your opponent tries to rise you can apply the maximum weight and concentration of strength to baulk his efforts (Fig. 11).

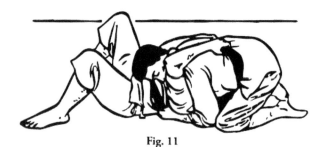

Fig. 11

KAMISHIHOGATAME
(UPPER LOCKING OF THE FOUR QUARTERS)
[With Both Arms Above]

Your opponent has fallen on his back and as before you are attacking him from behind his head.

You take up the initial squatting position, your knees spread to the necessary extent and resting on the mat and with your opponent's head held between your thighs.

Your right hand is inserted from his right upper armpit with fingers stretched, the palm on the mat or your hand grasping your opponent's back collar with the four fingers inside, and similarly your left hand is passed from his left upper armpit, fingers stretched and palm pressed on the mat or the hand gripping his back collar with the four fingers inside.

Your face may be turned optionally to the front, to right or left, and your head is placed upon your opponent's thorax. Your knees dig rather deeply into your opponent's back and you should try to concentrate your strength in the buttocks. With your chest you press down heavily upon your opponent's body. Alternatively your hand may grip your opponent's jacket at the back (Fig. 12).

Fig. 12

SHIHOGATAME
(LOCKING OF THE FOUR QUARTERS)
[Opponent's Left Arm Controlled With Belt]

Your opponent is supposed to have fallen to the side with his right shoulder undermost. You move round to the rear to attack him.

If then you thrust your left arm under his left back armpit it is possible that apprehending a Kansetsuwaza or Gyaku against his left arm he will take hold of your front belt or front collar and pull strongly on it. In that case you continue to thrust in deeply with your left arm so as to secure partial control of your opponent's body. Then with your right hand you pull strongly with a lifting sensation on his belt a little to the left of his hand grasping your front belt or front collar.

Next you transfer your hold to your left hand, making sure your grip is secure, and then with your right hand grasp his right side belt.

You sit down on your haunches but then open your thighs, stretch both legs and bring your opponent on to his back to facilitate execution of the Shihogatame.

While as a rule the hold on your opponent's belt is taken from the inside (*ura de*) it is admissible sometimes to use the regular or normal grip (*jun-ni-nigiru*) (Fig. 13).

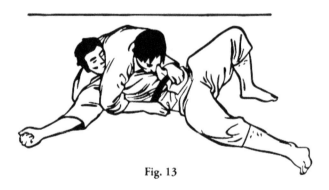

Fig. 13

YOKOSHIHOGATAME
(LATERAL LOCKING OF THE FOUR QUARTERS)

You attack in this case against your supine opponent's right side with your knees firmly planted on the mat.

Your right hand is passed from between your opponent's legs under his left thigh to grip his left side or back belt, and your left hand is passed from his right front shoulder underneath his neck to grip his back collar or left front collar.

Your knees are now opened as widely as possible and you should effect close contact between your chest and your opponent's right side chest and abdominal region. His right arm should be trapped between your left upper arm and left upper thigh.

Try to muster your weight and strength in the direction of the buttocks. Bear heavily with your chin in the space between your opponent's left side stomach and chest.

As in the case of all immobilization holds you must be ever ready to adapt the position of your legs to your opponent's movements as, for example, when he oscillates his body violently from side to side in his efforts to shake you off.

These adjustments may necessitate the stretching out of one leg or both legs, the elevation of your hips and so forth to baulk your opponent's counter technique. It goes without saying that for tactical reasons you may find it advisable to convert your Yokoshihogatame into, e.g. a Migi-Kesagatame, an Ushiro-Kesagatame or perhaps a Kamishihogatame. Such considerations are apposite in all cases and should never be overlooked (Fig. 14).

Fig. 14

Yokoshihogatame (effected with left arm under opponent's neck):

As before you are attacking your supine opponent from his right side. In this case, however, your right hand is passed under his left armpit and placed near his left shoulder while your left hand is passed under his right neck to grip his left front collar in the normal hold. Your jaw is pressed firmly against the space between his left neck and left shoulder. Your right leg is placed bent on the mat in contact with your opponent's right side stomach, and your left leg, also with bent knee, rests on the mat, and from this position you may succeed in immobilizing him (Fig. 15).

Fig. 15

VARIANTS IN USE OF RIGHT HAND:

(1) Your right hand may seize your opponent's left shoulder region.

(2) Your right hand may grasp your own left front collar.

(3) Your right hand may be passed from under your opponent's left armpit to his shoulder and placed thereon.

(4) Your right hand thrust from under his left armpit against his back may help to arrest his movements.

(5) Your right hand may be thrust into your opponent's back from his left side and grasp his right sleeve or your own right belt.

VARIANTS IN USE OF LEFT HAND:

Your left hand may be passed under your opponent's neck and linked with your right hand.

POSITION OF LEFT LEG:

(1) Your left leg may be rendered buoyant and your hips may be raised.

(2) Your left leg may be stretched to the rear and your left front waist brought in contact with the mat.

(3) You may alter the squatting position of your left leg to one in which the leg below the knee-joint is bent inwards.

POSITION OF RIGHT LEG:

The squatting position of your right leg may be modified by rising on tiptoe and disengaging your heel from under your buttocks.

Yokoshihogatame (with control of opponent's left armpit):

As before you attack your supine opponent from his right side. But in this approach you are lying on your stomach.

Your left hand is passed under his neck from his right side neck to grip his front collar, and your right hand from his right side chest is passed under his back to grasp his front collar near his left armpit, your thumb inside.

From your chest area and at right angles to your opponent's front chest your body should bear down heavily upon your opponent, your chin touching his left breast or thereabouts so that with both hands you can draw and constrict the root of his left arm. Concentrate your strength in your front waist and thus control your opponent (Fig. 16).

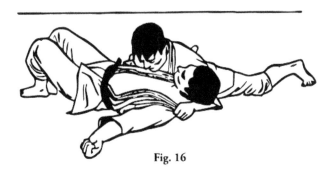

Fig. 16

The position of your legs may vary according to circumstances. They may assume approximately a squatting pose or be stretched out with the thighs widely separated in contact with the mat, perhaps with your right leg below the knee-joint turned inwards.

Yokoshihogatame (bending opponent's neck and torso):

Your opponent is lying on his back and you are as usual attacking him from his right side. Your left hand is thrust from his right side neck and under his neck to grip his left front collar from the direction of his back collar. Your right hand is passed over his stomach to effect a firm hold on his belt from the direction of his left side chest or it may be passed under his back so as to clasp him strongly.

Your right leg squats on the mat, with the knee-cap thrust against your opponent's buttocks from his right side hip. Your left leg is stretched out in close contact with the mat.

Tighten your left elbow and bend your opponent's neck to the left. Push with your right knee. Pull with your right hand clasping your opponent and bend his body as if trying to shape it like the Japanese Katakana syllable "ku" (<).

Your chin and chest should in much the same way as in the previous method press firmly against his body between his stomach and chest. Your strength should be concentrated in your left front waist. Thus you may succeed in immobilizing your opponent (Fig. 17).

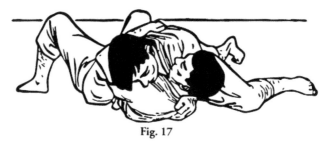

Fig. 17

Yokoshihogatame (with control of opponent's left hand):

You attack your supine opponent from his right side.

Your left hand is thrust from his right side under his neck and back collar to grip his left side collar. Your right hand is passed from his right side chest under his back to take hold of your opponent's left wrist. Then as you draw his hand in the direction of his right shoulder you lie on your stomach both legs outstretched and the tip of your toes raised on the mat, your chin pressed firmly against your opponent's torso between his front chest and left front shoulder.

From this description one infers that with your right hand hold on your opponent's left wrist, as you pull his arm strongly under his body towards his right shoulder you are to all intents and purposes applying a species of Catch hammerlock calculated to inflict pain upon your victim or even to menace his arm with dislocation (Fig. 18).

Fig. 18

One potential factor capable, in my opinion, of invalidating immobilization methods requiring the passage of your arm under your opponent's back is that, in the case of a heavyish man, you might find this movement far from easy to carry out. It would be necessary to take instant advantage of a moment when your opponent had slightly bridged his body in an effort to shake you off.

Yokoshihogatame (with control of opponent's left hand from above):

As before it is assumed that your opponent has fallen on his back and that you have moved round to his right side to make your attack.

You must effect close contact with his chest area at right angles from your chest to your abdominal region. Your right hand is threaded from his left armpit so that his left forearm is clamped between your right side neck and shoulder, while your left hand is passed from over his left shoulder under his left arm to grasp his left side belt. Your loins are lowered but with your legs conveniently spread to a degree compatible with retention of freedom of change (Henka).

Contact is established between your knee-caps and your opponent's right side stomach and chest area, a thrusting movement being imparted to your knees. With both your hands and arms you enfold your opponent's left arm, apply pressure with your knees, push strongly with the upper part of your body and in this manner seek to immobilize your opponent (Fig. 19).

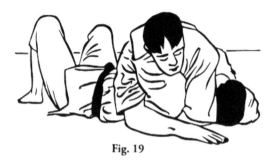

Fig. 19

VARIANTS IN USE OF HANDS AND ARMS:

(1) With your left hand and arm you may hold your opponent's left arm, and with your right hand grip the region of his left shoulder.

(2) Or with your right hand and arm you may hold his left arm, stretch your left arm and place it on the mat.

(3) Or with your right hand you may grip his left wrist and with your left hand passed from his left rear armpit hold your own right wrist or his left wrist and apply pressure.

KUZURE-YOKOSHIHOGATAME
(BROKEN LOCKING OF THE LATERAL FOUR QUARTERS)

This method presupposes the same relative positions, i.e. your opponent on his back and your attack initiated from his right side.

Your right knee is on the mat with the knee-cap thrust against his right side stomach, care being taken not to relax this contact. Your left hand is passed over from your opponent's left shoulder so as to grip his left side belt. Your left elbow must be kept taut. Your right hand is inserted between his front thighs to take hold optionally of his back mid belt or his trousers.

Unbroken contact must be maintained throughout between your left front chest and your opponent's front chest.

In order to perfect this method you must ever be on the alert to vary the position of your legs if need be in conformity with the Kesagatame or Ushiro-Kesagatame.

Also occasion may arise when you can effectively use both hands and arms freely to bend your opponent's body in the process of control (Fig. 20).

Fig. 20

KUZURE-KAMISHIHOGATAME
(BROKEN LOCKING OF THE UPPER FOUR QUARTERS)

Your opponent has fallen on his back and you have moved round to the back of his head to attack. Both your legs are extended to the rear.

Your left hand is passed from under his left shoulder to seize his right back belt midway with the thumb inside. Your right hand is passed from his right flank (under his back) to grasp his left side belt with the thumb inside. Both your elbows should closely adhere to his side chest. Your face is raised. The upper part of your body is bent somewhat backwards.

From your lower abdomen to your waist contact is maintained with the mat. The tip of your left foot is raised and your right foot is planted tiptoe on the mat. Your right side chest and front abdomen are pressed against your opponent's outer right arm. Your face may be turned somewhat to the left in contact with his left front waist. Now your left leg may be rendered "buoyant" and the sole of the foot pressed against the mat. In this way immobilization should be effected (Fig. 21).

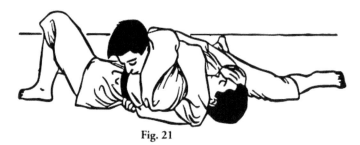

Fig. 21

VARIANT IN USE OF LEFT HAND:
Your left hand may grasp your opponent's left side belt.

VARIANTS IN USE OF RIGHT HAND:
(1) Your right hand may be passed from your opponent's upper right armpit to grip his back collar.

(2) It may be passed through his right upper armpit to grasp your own right front collar.

(3) It may grasp his right side belt.

(4) It may be passed from his right upper armpit, the palm extended and thrust against your opponent's back.

(5) Your palm may be extended and thrust under his right hip.

(6) You may take hold of the inner side of your opponent's trousers at the right knee-cap pressing from above so as to force his thighs apart.

(7) You may thrust your right hand against his back near the right side waist, grasp his trousers With the four fingers inside, with a drawing tightening action.

(8) Turning your right hand from the direction of his right hip to the buttocks you may grasp his trousers between the middle and the left side buttocks.

ANOTHER METHOD:

From the same relative positions with your left hand passed over your opponent's left shoulder you take old of his left side belt. Your right hand similarly grips his right side belt. Your left leg is stretched out with the inner side against the mat. Your right leg is held so that the knee is thrust obliquely against your opponent from his right shoulder to his back, and in close contact with the mat, your chin raised.

The weight of your body and your strength are concentrated in your front chest. Immobilization may thus be effected. Or your opponent's right arm can be held under your right armpit while with the four fingers inside you grip his back collar.

ANOTHER METHOD:

In this case both your knees are on the mat as you assume a squatting posture with your hips lowered. Your left hand is passed from your opponent's left rear side shoulder to grip his left side belt with the thumb inside. Your right arm gains control of his right arm by enfolding it under your right armpit from above so that your right hand can take hold of his back collar from the direction of his right side collar. Your four fingers are inside. Your face may be turned to right or left.

The weight and strength of your body seem to be concentrated in the direction of your buttocks as you press down heavily upon your opponent with your chest.

Kuzure-Kamishihogatame (with control of both opponent's armpits):

Your opponent has fallen turning sideways to the right and you have moved to the back to attack.

Your left hand is passed under his left back armpit to grip your own left front collar and your right hand under his right back armpit to grip his front collar. You lower your body to the rear.

Utilizing the strength of your left hand and your body you bring your opponent over on to his back and move your body towards his head. Both your legs are outstretched as you lie on your stomach.

Your opponent's back neck is held against your right shoulder, and as you concentrate your strength in your front waist you exert both your hands in as drawing constricting action. You should then contrive, if possible, to get your opponent's face and head under your front chest and push strongly against them thus immobilizing him (Fig. 22).

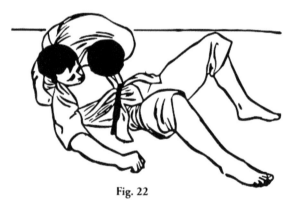

Fig. 22

Kuzure-Kamishihogatame (with control of opponent's neck):

As usual you are attacking your supine opponent from behind his head. Your right hand is inserted from over his right armpit so as to grasp his back collar with your four fingers inside, and your left hand and arm are wound tightly round his throat and left side neck so as to gain also a grasp of his back collar with your four fingers inside. Your opponent's face and head protrude to the outside of your left armpit. Both your legs are stretched to the rear with thighs comfortably separated. Your face is directed to your front. Your trunk from chest to stomach adheres to the mat.

Your weight and strength are assembled in your front waist. You pull and constrict to the rear with your right elbow. The upper part of our body is curved somewhat backwards with your left side chest you press against your opponent from his tight side face to his neck and in this manner effectively immobilize him (Fig. 23).

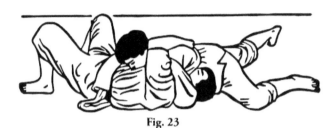

Fig. 23

VARIANTS IN USE OF LEFT HAND:
(1) Your left hand wound round your opponent's throat and left neck may sometimes be used to grip your own left or right front collar.

(2) Similarly, it may be used to grasp your own left front belt.

VARIANTS IN USE OF UPPER PART OF BODY:
(1) Your face may be turned somewhat to either left or right and your front chest pressed against your opponent's right front chest.

(2) Your right leg may assume a squatting position, your left leg opened to the aide. Your left arm enfolds your opponent's neck and your hand grasps your own left front belt. Your opponent's back neck is held against your left groin. As you apply a bending pressure raise your hips and lower your head and forehead.

VARIANTS IN USE OF LOWER LIMBS:
Your left leg may be opened to the side with the sole of the foot against the mat. Your right front waist is kept in contact with the mat.

UDEGARAMI or ENTANGLED ARMLOCK demonstrated by G. Whyman, 2nd Dan, against A. Bain, 1st. Dan

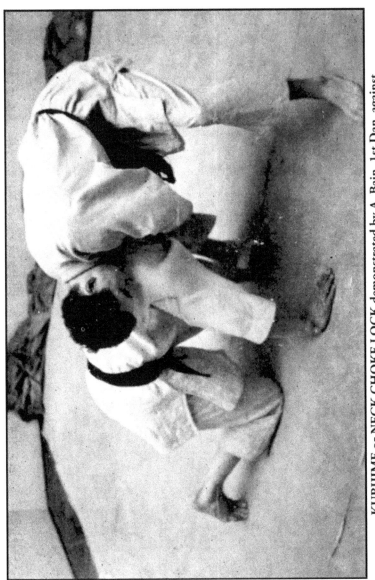

KUBIJIME or NECK CHOKE LOCK demonstrated by A. Bain, 1st Dan, against G. Whyman, 2nd Dan

TATE-SHIHOGATAME
(LENGTHWISE OR LONGITUDINAL LOCKING OF THE FOUR QUARTERS)

This is a superb immobilization method which will well repay study. As before your opponent is on his back. But in this case you must contrive to straddle his torso as though riding a horse—in the so-called equestrian position.

Your right hand is passed under your opponent's left armpit so as to grip his back collar with your four fingers inside and your left hand is passed under his right armpit to grip his back collar in the same way. The position of your legs is very important. Thus your right leg should be coiled round your opponent's left leg and your left leg round his right leg from the outside, as shown in the illustration.

The closest contact is established between your chest and abdomen and your opponent's chest and abdomen. But you should keep your body soft and pliant yet ever ready to foil your opponent's efforts to get up whether to right or left, as the case may be. In retort to these efforts you may spread the encircling legs whereby acute discomfort can be imparted to your opponent's legs. Care must be taken that he does not extricate either of his trapped legs from your scissor-like grip (Fig. 24).

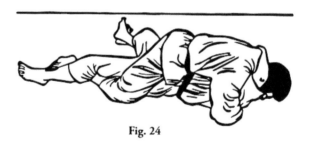

Fig. 24

VARIANTS IN USE OF HANDS:

Your left hand may be passed under your opponent's right armpit and your right hand from over his left neck. In that case with your left hand you hold his back collar with the four fingers inside and with your right hand take a similar hold, coordinating both hands in a tightening grip.

— Or else with your right hand you may grip your own left sleeve or your left or right front collar.

— Or it may be possible to gain control of your opponent along the lines of the Katagatame by pinning your opponent's right hand and arm between your own right shoulder and his right neck. In that case with your right hand you grip your own left collar with the four fingers inside and with your left hand your own jacket It the right elbow and apply constricting action.

— Or with your left hand you may grip your opponent's left side collar, thumb inside, your lower arm against his throat, While with your right hand thrust from his left side neck Ind past his back neck you take hold of your own jacket at the left elbow so that your opponent's throat and neck from front and back are subjected to crushing pressure as in the case of a genuine stranglehold.

It is interesting to compare Oda's version of the Tate-Shihogatame with that advocated by Takahiko Ishikawa, 7th Dan, former All-Japan Champion. The latter's method does not concern itself so much with your opponent's legs but concentrates on control of his body from the hips upward. Thus you are instructed, after having got astride his torso, to pass your left hand from over his *left* shoulder so as to gain hold of his back *belt* with your thumb inside, while you pass your right hand under his left armpit and under his left forearm so as to stretch his left arm upwards and bring the inner side of his wrist against your own right shoulder, while simultaneously you grip your own left front collar with your right hand, thumb inside.

Then in sharp contra-distinction to Oda's method you adjust your legs near your opponent's *armpits* at either side. The upper part of your body is lowered to the front and prostrated obliquely over his left shoulder until your head actually presses against the mat.

On the other hand, the late veteran Hidekazu Nagaoka, 10th Dan, and Kaichiro Samura, 10th Dan, in their description of the Tate-Shihogatame, state that your right hand and arm are inserted from over your opponent's left shoulder and under his neck while your left hand and arm are similarly threaded over his right shoulder and under his neck. Both elbows are held so that they jut out at either side to right and left. Your head is pressed against the side of your opponent's right shoulder while the tip of your own right shoulder is placed against his neck and throat below the chin.

These several methods simply go to confirm the validity of the argument against standardization in Judo and the advisability of leaving a wide margin for the exercise of individual initiative and adaptation to ever-changing circumstances.

KUZURE-TATE-SHIHOGATAME
(BROKEN LONGITUDINAL OR LENGTHWISE LOCKING OF
THE FOUR QUARTERS)

For the application of this method you should straddle your opponent's upturned body from his abdominal region to his chest. Then your left hand is passed from over his right shoulder under his back so as to take hold of his belt at a point between the middle and the right side. Then as you apply tension with this hold you pass your right hand from his left armpit and under his forearm so as to grip your own front collar. Your right elbow is tightened, and your opponent's left arm is brought into a position resembling the Udegatame or Armlock.

Now your left leg is bent and thrust against his back from his right side neck as you squat on the calf, while your right leg presses against his back from his left side stomach. Your face is turned to the right. Your buttocks are raised and your left chest is lowered. Your body as a whole lies upon your opponent obliquely to his left. Both your feet hold him firmly scissor-wise and in this way you immobilize both the upper part of his body and his left arm (Fig. 25).

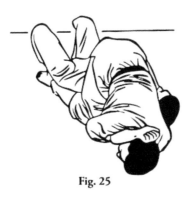

Fig. 25

ANOTHER METHOD:

You are as before astride your opponent bearing down strongly upon his chest and abdomen. Your left hand is passed from his right back neck to seize your own left front belt or side belt. Your right hand is inserted into his left armpit so as to hug his left forearm and then take hold of your own right front collar. You tighten your elbow. Your left leg is bent and in a squatting position thrust against your opponent from his right side neck into his back.

Your right leg is also thrust into his back from his left side stomach. Your face is turned to the right, your buttocks are raised, your left front chest is lowered.

Contact is established between your body and your opponent obliquely to his left. Both your legs retain their firm grip on his torso. Your left elbow containing his neck is drawn backwards, and a bending action applied to his neck, so that immobilization is effected.

ANOTHER METHOD:

As before your legs contain your opponent and you control his torso. Your right hand passes under his left armpit to hug his forearm. Your left hand passes from over his right upper back shoulder and grasps the right wrist of your hand hugging his left forearm or you interlock both your hands. You tighten your left elbow. Your face is turned to your left. The upper part of your body is thrust against your opponent obliquely to his left. Your right front chest is lowered and you control your opponent's left arm. Immobilization is thus effected.

ANOTHER METHOD:

From the same starting position your left hand is passed from over your opponent's left shoulder under his back armpit to grip his left side belt. Your left leg is dug from his right side neck into his back or contact is effected with his right side chest. Your right leg is thrust against your opponent from his left side stomach to his chest.

As in the method described by Ishikawa your forehead is pressed again the mat. With your left side neck held so that your opponent's left forearm is brought parallel with the mat you press strongly in the direction of his left neck. The palm of your right hand is spread on his left side and in this manner full control is effected.

This hold-down may conceivably cause pain in your opponent's left shoulder and so compel surrender. The facility with which this method, among others, can be converted into a Gyaku is a favourite attribute from the standpoint of attack.

UKIGATAME
(FLOATING LOCK)

Your opponent is lying on his back and you are attacking from his right side.

With your left hand you take hold of his right outer sleeve midway and with your right hand his left front collar.

Note that in this approach you do not try to lie on your opponent but are leaning over him with your knees bent. Contact must be effected with your opponent from your right ankle to knee-cap and from his right front armpit to his chest lightly and obliquely. With your left hand you draw and lift your opponent and right hand press against him.

In this manner immobilization may be effected (Fig. 26).

Fig. 26

SANKAKU-OSAEKOMI
(TRIANGULAR IMMOBILIZATION)

Your opponent is lying on his back and you have straddled his torso.

Your legs grip him on either side high up against his thorax in a fashion somewhat arbitrarily called "triangular".

His left hand and arm are placed midway between your right shoulder and right side neck; you stretch his left arm and thrust with your right shoulder and as you bend over your opponent with your head on the mat and exert both your arms, an effective Kansetsu-waza, specifically an Udegatame or armlock may result (Fig. 27).

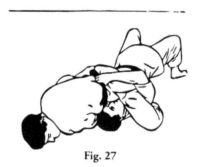

Fig. 27

GYAKU-SANKAKU-OSAEKOMI
(GYAKU-TRIANGULAR IMMOBILIZATION)

It is assumed in this case that your opponent is inexperienced in Groundwork and is trying ineffectively to apply the Yokoshihogatame or Lateral Locking of the Four Quarters and that you are lying under him.

In that case you should with your left hand against his left side neck push him strongly in the direction of your feet. Then your left leg should be passed across his left side neck and hooked behind it. Your right leg is then raised and the knee-joint hitched to your left ankle. Then as you constrict and tighten both thighs and bend them as it were towards your right heel, a species of Sankakujime or triangular chokelock, to be described more in detail in Chapter VII results, and your opponent is unable to get up.

In that case you should seize his left leg (with your right hand) and capsize him to your left side. If he falls on to his back you should act as in the case of the original Sankaku-Osaekomi already described, using both legs and clasping your opponent's waist with both arms (Fig. 28).

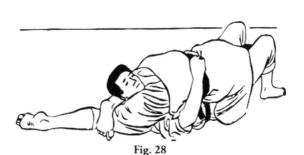

Fig. 28

CHAPTER IV
PRINCIPLE OF VARIANT (HENKA) AND METHODS OF ENTRY OR HAIRIKATA IN OSAEKOMIWAZA

THE principle of the variant or change (Henka in Japanese) is, of course, fundamental in all branches of Judo but in none more so perhaps than in Osaekomiwaza with which we are at present dealing. Adaptation to the situation and utilization of opportunity may be regarded as almost synonymous terms. Lacking grasp of this principle and its practical application the Judoka may not hope to excel in his exposition of the art. Nor can this enviable objective be easily attained. The almost reflex ability to apply a variant or Henka calls for the rare combination of such qualities, alike mental and physical, as presence of mind, willpower, precision and subtlety. The path to development of these qualities may well prove long and arduous and entail much apparently wasted effort during the earlier experimental stages.

At the outset the tyro may feel daunted by the seemingly endless diversity and complexity of these variants. Thus there are variants applicable to Osaekomiwaza, Shimewaza, and Kansetsuwaza respectively. To enumerate them in detail would be virtually impossible, although already in the preceding chapter some of the principal ones appertaining to Osaekomiwaza have been specified. But in the practice of Katamewaza generally the aspiring Judoka must ever be prepared to switch in almost a split second from, say, Osaekomiwaza to Shimewaza or vice versa, or from Shimewaza to Kansetsuwaza or vice versa, for often the line of demarcation between these three branches of Katamewaza is very tenuous indeed. "Thin partitions do their bounds divide." And in the swift choice of variants pertinent to these ever-changing situations a good deal must be left to individual initiative and improvisation. The author speaks about variants or Henka being reflected in the eye or felt in the heart, or natural variants or special kinds of variants, and among all these variants the presence of fixed or definite stages is conceivable. The student may advantageously begin with the less violent of these variants and thus empirically exemplify the Spenserian definition of progress, i.e. transition from the homogeneous to the heterogeneous.

METHODS OF ENTRY OF HAIRIKATA:

Success in Osaekomiwaza, as indeed in the other two branches of Katamewaza, may be said to depend largely upon your ability to detect any weakness in your opponent's defences and to take instant advantage of it. What is more, the Katamewaza specialist does not confine his attacks to a supine or prostrate opponent but perfects methods of bringing a standing one to the mat without infringing the rule which forbids you merely to drag him crudely downwards.

It must be admitted, from study of the Oda methods, that the dividing line between the permissible and prohibited is often difficult to detect, while generally speaking the overall inductive evidence proves conclusively that many of the earlier bans have latterly been scrapped and that far greater latitude than formerly is nowadays extended to Judoka in the use of both legs and arms in order to extort submission. In any case, unless and until the Judoka has acquired a sizable repertoire of these so-called Hairikata or methods of entry, he will remain gravely handicapped when pitted against an antagonist his superior in this technique of groundwork.

It is hardly too much to say that the yardstick whereby the relative merit of Osaekomiwaza can be gauged and contrasted with other branches of the art is the Judoka's skill in swiftly resorting to the Hairikata best adapted to application of the contemplated immobilization method. To this end unremitting study and training must be devoted. At the outset, however, the average Judoka is likely to be most interested in techniques comparatively easy of application and at the same time best calculated to prove effective in contest.

The first object of every Judoka in contest is to adopt a posture calculated to prove most advantageous to himself and most disadvantageous to his opponent whether in defence or attack, and his opponent should in his turn have at his disposal a fund of knowledge covering the most likely methods of both defence and attack he will be called upon to nullify in order in his turn to effect an entry and immobilize the other fellow. Although it is manifestly impossible to provide for all eventualities, our author has listed for purposes of reference eight styles of defence most frequently resorted to by an opponent against an attack which aims at immobilizing him. These styles are alphabetically designated as follows:

A-style: Your opponent has fallen on his back. With his left hand he grips your left lapel and with his right hand your left ankle or the bottom of your trousers. His right foot is placed against your left front waist and as he pulls with both hands he thrusts strongly with his right foot. His left foot is planted against your right front chest or front waist or is hitched into your right knee-joint in anticipation of your offensive variant.

B-style: Your opponent passes his right leg from the inside of your right front thigh so that from below the knee-joint he hooks it from above. Then he hooks the back part of his left knee-joint into his right ankle and his left ankle is linked from below your right ankle with the toes bent and stretched backward so that your right leg is clipped and stretched and unable to extricate itself. Occasionally he may grip your trousers at the right knee with his right hand and push against them.

C-style: Your opponent hooks your right leg from the outside with his left leg, the toes bent backwards. His right leg is passed from the inside of your right front thigh so that the rear side of the knee-joint links up with his left ankle. His right ankle passes from under your right ankle, toes bent backwards, and hooks and stretches your right ankle so that you cannot easily extricate it.

D-style: Your opponent passes his right leg from the inner side of your left leg so as to entangle it from the outside. He raises his left leg and links the knee-joint with his right ankle. The toes are thrust in the direction of your buttocks. With both hands he grips your front belt and draws strongly on it. He stretches his right leg and thus defends himself.

E-style: Your opponent from below passes his right leg from your inner side outside your left leg so as to coil round the outer side. His foot is placed against your front belt. His left foot is raised and also placed against your front belt. With both hands from above he takes hold of your front belt, stretches both legs and pulls strongly with both hands to defend himself.

F-style: You are assumed to be on your back. Your opponent has adopted a squatting attitude between your thighs. With his right hand he seizes your left side belt and with his left hand your right side belt. His face is turned to the front and placed against your abdominal region. He pulls strongly with both hands as though trying to bend your body.

G-style: Again you are supposed to be lying on your back. With his left arm your opponent pins your right leg in his left armpit from the knee-joint to the ankle, and grips his own right front collar (?with that hand). With his right hand he grasps and presses your front belt. He kneels with his right knee on the mat and the left knee raised. In this way he tries to control your freedom of action.

H-style: Your opponent has embraced you from behind and with both legs has scissored your torso for the evident purpose of attacking with a strangle-hold.

I-style: Your opponent has scissored your torso between his legs (from underneath). With his right hand he grasps and pulls your back belt. With his left arm he pins your right arm and with his left hand grasps your left side collar in contemplation of a necklock or Gyaku.

We now pass on to a selection of the more effective ways of Hairikata or entry methods.

Method Of Throwing Opponent By Seizing His Leg:

You are both assumed to be engaged in the Shizentai or Natural Posture. Your opponent with his right hand and you with the left hand are employing the normal hold. At the moment when your opponent is about to seize you with his left hand you bend forward the upper part of your body; with your right hand you take hold of your opponent's right leg from the inside and under the knee-joint to the ankle and from your front lift it violently. Simultaneously with your left hand you push your opponent so that he is thrown towards his right back corner.

It ought not to be necessary to impress upon you the importance of reinforcing all your bodily movements in every instance with the power emanating from your *saika tanden* or lower abdomen, as explained in *The Manual of Judo.*

Method Of Throwing Opponent By Clasping Him From Behind:

It may happen that failing to bring off a throw your opponent has his back turned to you. In that case with your left hand from behind you should grasp his left front collar and with your right hand his right front collar. Then hanging on to him you hook him in front from the outside left back with your left foot, and as you fall yourself contrive to throw him on his back.

Then from the all-fours position you endeavour to get in to effect immobilization.

Entry Method By Grasping Opponent's Back Belt And Capsizing Yourself:
If your opponent happens to be on all-fours or on his stomach, move round to his head. Thrust your left hand from under his right front armpit to his back. With your right hand grip his back belt midway and as you draw strongly on it instill counter-action or recoil into your body and capsize yourself to the left side so that your opponent is brought over on to his back. Then instantly on all-fours or on your stomach switch round from your opponent's head to his left side and mounting him from above effect entry for immobilization. In this case too your left hand may be passed over his right shoulder and hold his right arm from above.

Entry Method By Pulling Down And Sutemi:
You are both engaged in Tachiwaza. Should it chance that your opponent's right hand and your own left hand grip each other, instantly with your free right hand take hold of your opponent from his right front to his back collar and uninterruptedly pull him downwards to his right front corner. As he staggers throw yourself, while pulling, in the direction of your right back corner and with both hands suddenly pull, turn and lift your opponent and land him on his back preparatory to your entry for an immobilization attack.

Entry Method By Overturning Opponent To Your Right Side:
You are both engaged in either the Shizentai or Jigotai. Without delay seize your opponent's left side collar with your left hand and with your right hand his left outer sleeve midway. Hook your right leg into his right knee-joint from in front and above, and passing your left leg from his thigh hook the back of the ankle in his knee-joint.

Although the author fails to say so, it must be assumed that at this stage you are hanging on to your opponent with both your hands, since both your feet are no longer on the mat! You pull your opponent down with both hands and at the same time with your left leg from below spring lift him to your right so that he falls on his back to your right side, whereupon withdrawing your left leg you instantly get on top of him to effect immobilization.

Methods Of Attack Against A Supine Opponent:

A falling opponent can land in three main postures, ie. on his back, on his side and on all-fours. But the potential moves of hands and feet are almost countless. Your hands grip, pull, push, clasp, hook, etc., and your legs and feet are flexed, they push, pull, stretch, hook, attach, encircle, entangle, etc., in endless combinations. And upon the manner in which you manipulate your hands and feet the issue of victory or defeat will depend.

Moreover during contest one is usually excited and apt to miss opportunities for recourse to the relevant method. Therefore it cannot be too often insisted that only by dint of seemingly endless repetitions in Randori can the zealous Judoka hope to become truly proficient in Katamewaza generally and Osaekomiwaza more particularly.

Method Of Entry By Gripping Opponent's Feet:

You attack from a half-sitting posture. With your right hand you grasp your opponent's right ankle and with your left hand his left ankle and as you drag him along the mat you oscillate them violently and try to effect an entry from either side.

Method Of Entry By Controlling Opponent's Knees:

Again you are in a half-sitting posture. With your right hand you take hold of your opponent's trousers above his left knee, and with your left hand a similar hold of his trousers over his right knee. While pushing somewhat downwards you switch your body to the right, pull and raise both your hands to the right side, detach both your opponent's feet from your front waist, contrive to emerge at his right side and without relinquishing your double hold of his trousers at the knees bring your right knee into contact with his front abdominal area; then sinking the upper part of your body break in to effect immobilization.

Method Of Entry By Gripping Opponent's Trousers:

Again you are in a half-sitting posture. With your right hand you take hold of the bottom of your opponent's left leg trousers and with your left hand a similar grip of the bottom of his right leg trousers. You draw both your hands close together and then with your right hand only retain your hold of both his right and left leg trousers. Switch your body to the right and getting round to your opponent's right side enter for immobilization.

Method Of Entry By Detaching Opponent's Left Leg:

At first your opponent with his left hand grasps your left side collar and pulls strongly on it. His right foot is applied to your left front waist and thrusts against it. With his right hand he grips the bottom of your left leg trousers or hooking it in your left ankle extends his line of defence.

Continuing he may exchange his left foot for his right and with his right leg reap your right leg from the inner side in an attempt to throw you to the rear. Guarding yourself against this danger you should with both hands grasp his left ankle or his trousers, pull to the right and detach his foot from your left front waist. With your right leg you cross his right leg and as you come out at his right side you get in for immobilization.

Method Of Entry By Gripping Opponent's Front Collar With Your Right Hand And Switching Your Body To The Left:

Your opponent has applied both feet to your front and holding your right front collar with his left is acting on the defensive. You are in a half-sitting posture. With your left hand you grip his right front and simultaneously with the switching of your body the left with your right hand you suddenly drag and lift your opponent and while blocking him in a position between sitting and getting up, quickly substitute right hand for your left hand hold on his right front collar which you pull towards the mat, and from this try to immobilize him.

Method Of Entry By Jumping Over Opponent's Knees:

Kneeling on the mat you place your left hand upon your opponent's right knee and your right hand upon his left knee and then utilizing both his knees as a vaulting-horse you leap over them and getting astride of his stomach seek to immobilize him.

Method Of Entry By Dragging And Lifting Opponent:

With your left hand you grasp his right outer sleeve midway and with your right hand take a similar hold of his left outer sleeve midway. Then as you drag and lift him you straddle his torso and go in for immobilization.

Method Of Entry By Creeping Upwards:

Your opponent has applied both feet to your front waist and is thrusting hard against it. If now you stretch out both your legs behind the resistance of his feet is nullified. On your part you should contrive to get both his legs under your chest and abdominal region, and as you push against them clasp them with both arms from above and by degrees creep upwards, as it were, from his legs to his waist and chest with the object of applying an immobilization hold.

Method Of Entry By Reciprocally Stepping Across Each Other's Legs:
Your opponent is on his back and you are standing up, but neither of you has taken hold of the other. Now if with your right leg you step over your opponent's right outer thigh, being on his guard against a fresh advance of your right leg he may hook it with his left leg. Then with your left leg you may step over his left outer thigh when he may with his right leg this time try to obstruct you. After several repetitions of this manoeuvre your opponent may show signs of weariness when taking advantage of an opening you may be able to effect an entry.

Method Of Entry By Jumping Over While Switching Body To The Right;
Your opponent has pushed both feet severally against your front waist. You apply your left arm from the elbow to the fingertips to a spot midway between your opponent's left shoulder and neck and simultaneously switching your body to the right leap upwards and in this way nullify the effect of the pressure of your opponent's feet against your front waist. This diversion may afford you a chance to get in for an immobilization hold.

Method Of Entry By Gripping Front Belt With Both Hands:
Your opponent is on his back and defending himself in A-style which means that with his left hand he grips your left lapel and with his right hand your left ankle or the bottom of your trousers. His right foot is placed against your left front waist and as he pulls with both hands he thrusts strongly with his right foot. His left foot is planted against your right front chest or front waist or is hitched into your right knee-joint.

In retort with your left hand you grip your opponent's front belt with the so-called front or outside hold (*omote*) in which your four fingers from above the belt are looped under it with the thumb inside, while with your right hand you take hold of the left approach to his front belt using the reverse or *ura* grip in which your four fingers from below are looped over his belt and your thumb is also on the outside.

With both hands you strongly push his front waist downwards. Assuming a kneeling position with the left knee on the mat and using your left elbow you push downwards from your opponent's right knee to his thigh from the inside.

From this point the author's description lacks clarity. Thus he speaks about your shin—which one not stated—touching your opponent's thigh—which one not stated—and about your leg—which one not stated—being applied to your opponent's shin from his knee to his ankle.

The ends of your toes are hitched from the bottom of his ankle and protrude to the front and the freedom of his right leg is controlled. Your right elbow is extended and thrust midway between your opponent's right leg and right hip. Passing over his right thigh you remove your left leg and winding it under his loin (right) effect an entry. In this case when you have controlled your opponent's right leg and are trying to get in, your opponent may bend his left knee and apply it crosswise to the side of your front waist thus obstructing your entry.

You should in that event let go your right hand hold on his belt and from above his left thigh insert your hand between his right side waist and thigh, switch your body to the right and at the same time withdraw your waist, grasp your opponent's ankle with your right hand and endeavour to get in.

Method Of Entry By Controlling Opponent's Knee And Turning The Body:

Your opponent has assumed the typical A-style defensive position already described. With your left hand you grasp his trousers above the right knee and with your right hand similarly grasp his trousers above the left knee. As you switch your body to the right with both hands you drag him to the right side, then at once advance your right foot to the region of his right groin. With your hands holding his trouser knees you push them aside and get in.

After advancing your right foot to your opponent's right groin it may be possible to take hold of his thigh and adopt a stance preparatory to a Rear Scarf Hold or Ushirogesa. You gradually extend your legs and turn your back on your opponent as a preliminary move in this direction.

Method Of Entry To Left Side By Grasping Left Cuff And Trousers:

Your opponent applies both feet to your front waist and thrusts against it. You are in a half-sitting position.

With your right hand you take hold of his left cuff and with your left hand the end of his left trousers. Then as you switch your body to the left you drag your opponent along the mat, advance your left leg between his left armpit and torso, and establish contact between your left knee and his chest and abdominal area. With your left hand, the fingers inside, you grip his left side collar or back collar, bring the upper part of your body in contact with his chest and abdomen, and in this way try to effect an opening for immobilization.

Method Of Entry By Dragging Opponent By Both Lapels:

You have gone round to your opponent's head. He is supposed to have raised both feet over his head and thrust them or his knees against you from your chest to lower abdomen. With your left hand, the fingers inside, you grasp his left side lapel, and with your right hand, the fingers inside, his right side lapel. Then using both hands you strongly drag and lift him and simultaneously drawing yourself up displace your opponent's thrusting feet.

Availing yourself of this opening you bring your chest and abdominal region heavily down upon your opponent from behind his head and so pave the way to immobilization.

Method Of Entry By Shifting Back Opponent's Left Leg:

You are supposed to be on all-fours or squatting at your opponent's feet, the left one of which has been hitched on to your right shoulder. With your left hand you grip his right trousers above the thigh and inserting your right hand from the inner side of his left thigh you seize his front belt. Then shifting back his left leg to the left side you get in for immobilization.

Method Of Entry By Retracting Hip To Left:

You are assumed to be at close quarters with your opponent's hips. Passing your left hand from over his right thigh you grip his trousers at the inner side of the thigh, and inserting your right hand from the inner side of his left thigh you grasp his left side belt.

Taking care that he does not thrust both feet into the area between your chest and stomach, get in between his thighs, extend your right hand from his left side belt over his right side collar to grip his back collar with the thumb inside; retract your hips to the left, press his left leg in the direction of his right shoulder, establish contact between your right side chest to the hip and your opponent's body from his left outside thigh to the hip, pushing downwards. Your face is turned to the left side.

Letting his left leg go you apply your right wrist to his throat, concentrating your weight against it so that he experiences discomfort from an embryo necklock.

Method Of Entry By Carrying Opponent's Left Leg On Shoulder:

You are in a squatting position between your opponent's thighs. With your right hand, thumb inside, you grip his back collar from the direction of his right side collar, the wrist against his throat. Pushing against it with that hand, with your left hand you seize his left front collar and draw it towards you, your face turned to the left. With your right shoulder you press your opponent's left leg in the direction of his right shoulder so that his neck is brought into a strangulation position. His left leg spontaneously slips from your right shoulder as you get in to immobilize him.

Lobster Attack Method:

You are in a squatting position between your opponent's thighs. Your right hand is inserted from his left inner thigh to seize his left side belt and your left hand is similarly inserted from his right inner thigh to grasp his right side belt. Your face is turned to the front with your chin tucked into your chest and you effect light contact with your opponent's abdominal region.

Separating both his legs you adjust them so that they cannot thrust against your stomach from the knees downwards. You strongly pull your opponent with both hands, and then as you rise up you drag him along the mat and press down upon him with your front chest imparting a bent shape to his body. Then with your right hand you take hold of his left front collar and with your left hand a grip lower down with the thumb inside so that your left wrist touches his throat.

Concentrating the strength and weight of your body you switch your hips to the right and maintaining contact between your left side chest and your opponent's stomach, turning your face to the right and pushing downwards you expose his throat to strangulation. Moreover his cervical muscles are subjected to great strain and he experiences considerable pain.

As he shifts himself forward his right leg slips from your left shoulder and you get in. In this so-called lobster attack method, as you drag your opponent along the mat with both hands and by subjecting his cervical muscles to painful pressure effect control over him, you may seize his back belt midway with your right hand, thumb inside; next with your left hand grip his back collar from his left side collar so that your wrist constricts his larynx.

Method Of Entry By Controlling Right Wrist:

When you are applying the lobster attack method to your opponent and are dragging him along the mat, he may hitch his left hand in your right ankle or heel and hang on to it. In that case take hold of his left wrist or sleeve and pull and bend it in the direction of his left shoulder, and as his right leg slips from your left shoulder contrive to come out at his right side and attempt to immobilize him.

Method Of Entry By Crossing Over Opponent's Right Knee:

Your opponent has fallen on his back. You pass your right hand from his left inner thigh to seize his left side belt. With your left arm you clasp his right thigh from above and take hold of his trousers, draw in your chin, turn your face to the front and apply it lightly to your opponent's abdominal region.

Then in a flash you cross over his right knee; with your left hand you pull his trousers tightly to the back and place your body on top of his knee and gradually enter; or while you push his right knee with your left hand you enter; or clasping your opponent and with your left front shoulder as centre and holding your body pancake-wise you cross over his right knee and enter; or with your left hand applied to your opponent's knee-cap you cross over, change to your right hand, hold his left waist and enter. The action of crossing over your opponent's knee is effected with buoyancy as though you were vaulting without the use of your legs!

Should your opponent have encircled your torso with his legs and you then disentangle them, he may take advantage of an opportunity to bend his legs and thrust them against your chest. You ought therefore to be prepared for such an eventuality.

METHODS OF ATTACK AGAINST OPPONENT WHO HAS FALLEN SIDEWAYS

Method Of Entry By Hooking Left Hand In Neck:

You move round to your opponent's right side, lower your loins, hitch your left hand into his right side neck from below, bring your right hand to his left side, push him with the upper part of your body and force him over on to his back to effect immobilization.

Method Of Entry By Grasping Shoulder And Trousers And Overturning Opponent:

You move round to your opponent's rear side in a half-sitting posture. With your right hand you take hold of his jacket at the left shoulder or left elbow and with your left hand his left leg trousers or your left hand from his right rear thigh can be hitched into his left leg and used to overturn him. This description is hardly so clear as it might be!

Method Of Entry By Thrusting Right Hand Into Left Armpit:

You move round to your opponent's head. From that direction you thrust your right hand into his left armpit and with your left hand grasp his left side belt, then suddenly turn him over to the left flank on to his back.

Method Of Entry By Thrusting In Right Hand And Retracting Loins:

You move round to your opponent's head and rest your right knee on the mat. Your right hand is thrust from the direction of his head into his left armpit towards his back while simultaneously with your left hand you take hold of his left side or back belt. You now raise your right knee and advance it to your opponent's right flank. With your right hand you thrust more and more deeply. Then again you kneel on your right knee, bring your left leg to the rear, retract your loins to the right, push against your opponent with the upper part of your body and bring him over to his back.

Method Of Entry By Controlling Left Hand With Belt:

Your opponent has fallen sideways with his right shoulder underneath. You move round in the direction of his head. Your left hand is hitched deeply into his left back armpit. With both legs you firmly encircle his chest and abdominal region and so control his torso.

Fearing gyaku against his left arm he may with his left hand grip his own front belt in defence. With your right hand you take hold of his jacket near his left hand grip, pulling strongly; then transfer the hold to your left hand, stretch both your legs, bring the upper part of your body into contact with your opponent's chest and stomach and get him over on to his back.

Method Of Entry By Gripping Opponent's Right Elbow And Stretching:

When your opponent has fallen sideways you move round to his rear and take up a squatting position. In the first place with your right hand you catch his left hand from the shoulder and pull and stretch it, and if he begins in some degree to incline on to his back you bring the upper part of your body into contact with his body from his left front shoulder to his chest and simultaneously gripping his right elbow with both hands pull him on to his back.

Method Of Entry While Strangling Opponent:

Your opponent is lying sideways. You have intersected your arms as though preparatory to applying a chokelock or gyaku against which your opponent is defending himself. You move round to his back.

Your left hand is thrust from under his left back armpit and takes hold of your own left front or side collar, and your right arm is wound round his throat from his right back neck, the thumb inside. Your opponent sags somewhat.

With your right arm pressure is applied to his neck and throat and as your body is lowered, if you pull his left arm your opponent naturally lies on his back. You place the upper part of your body upon his left arm which is held against your chest.

This method of entry is described as a combination method or Kenyoho. It sometimes happens that the arm which your opponent is using in defence helps to choke him!

Method Of Entry By Inserting Hand From Opponent's Front Thigh:

When your opponent is lying sideways to the right you move round to his front. With your left hand you take hold of his jacket at the back near his left shoulder or back belt. Your left front chest and shoulder are held against his left front chest and shoulder. Your right hand is inserted from his front thigh, the upper part of your body falls forward; with your right hand you switch his left leg and bring him on to his back.

Method Of Entry By Overturning Opponent Onto His Back:

When your opponent is lying sideways on his right you shift round in the direction of his head. Your left hand is inserted from his left back armpit and grips your own left front collar. Both your legs are stretched and as you lie on your stomach you pull and turn your opponent on to his back. Your front chest is placed upon his front chest in preparation for a hold-down.

Method Of Entry By Combination Of Shime And Gyaku:

When your opponent is lying on his right side you take up a position with your left knee on the mat (apparently behind your opponent, although the author does not say so). Your left hand is thrust from under your opponent's left rear armpit and grips your own left front collar. Your right foot is planted in your opponent's right front armpit.

As you fall on your back you apply your right back thigh to his throat. Your left leg passing his back is stretched and the knee-joint hooked in your right ankle assuming the so-called triangle (*sankaku*) shape. Your opponent fearing gyaku on his left arm grasps his own front belt for defence. In that case you utilize the method described in the method of entry by controlling his left hand and belt, i.e. with your right hand you take hold of his jacket near his left hand grip pulling strongly, and then relaxing your leg hold raise yourself and effecting contact between your own and your opponent's chest get on top of him to execute a hold-down.

When you are immobilizing your opponent with the Sankaku-Osaekomi (Triangular Hold-down described in Chapter III), with your right hand you grip his right side lapel with the thumb inside, stretch your legs and pulling strongly with your right hand perhaps enforce surrender. Or again, with your right hand you may seize your opponent's left wrist and pluck away the hand holding his belt and clamping that arm between your left shoulder and neck apply an Udegatame (Armlock) variant.

If your opponent opens his left armpit your right hand can be thrust from it and hitched into the wrist of his left hand holding his front belt and together with your left hand twist and raise his left hand in the direction of his back to apply a Gyaku. This form of entry can be very effective in contest.

Method Of Entry By Overturning Opponent To Direct Back:

Your opponent is prostrate in a seated posture. You straddle his back from behind, insert your right hand from under his right back armpit and take hold of his right front collar, and with your left hand passed under his left back armpit you grasp his left front collar, then with the combined momentum of your body and the tension of your hand hold you bring your opponent over to his direct rear so that you can effect an entry.

Method Of Entry By Hooking Both Hands In Opponent's Elbow:

Your opponent is on his stomach and you move round to his right side to attack. You are kneeling on the mat.

Passing your right hand from above underneath his chin you hook his left elbow and similarly passing your left hand from under his right armpit hook the same elbow. Your jaw is applied to his back and the upper part of your body pushed out to the front. Simultaneously you draw both your hands towards yourself and bring your opponent over on to his back.

This method bears a strong family resemblance to one used in Catch-as-Catch-Can to get one's opponent on to his back and shoulders.

Method Of Entry By Rotating Opponent's Body:

When your opponent is on his stomach you straddle his torso. Your right hand is passed under his right back armpit and takes hold of his front collar and your left hand under his left armpit and grasps his left front collar. Apparently with the help of this joint hold and your knees you drag and lift your opponent along the mat, and almost simultaneously encircle his trunk with your legs and capsize him to the side or direct rear. Your left hand is deeply thrust in from his left arm to his back neck; your right leg is stretched and extricated from under his body.

When your body has been placed upon his stomach you withdraw your right hand and transfer your right leg to the direction of his right side. Then, continuing, you move your right hand to his right flank and shifting in the direction of his head effect an entry for a hold-down.

Method Of Entry By Capsizing Self:

When your opponent is on all-fours or on his stomach you move round to his head with both knees on the mat. Your right hand is passed under his left back armpit and grasps his right front collar with the thumb inside. Your left hand is passed from his right back armpit, and the back of the wrist brought in contact with his back neck and as you thrust with it reaction is brought into play and you capsize yourself to the left side bringing your opponent over on to his back when your chest is imposed upon his chest to facilitate a hold-down.

Method Of Entry By Overturning Opponent From Rear Thigh:

When your opponent is on all-fours or on his stomach you move round to his left side; then with your left hand you grip his back collar or his jacket at the right elbow and passing your right hand from under his rear thighs take hold of his front belt; then strongly lifting him overturn him on to his back.

Method Of Entry By Utilizing Shime And Overturning Opponent:

Again when your opponent is on all-fours or on his stomach, you move round to his right side, both knees on the mat. Your left hand is passed under his right back armpit and with the four fingers inside you grasp his left side collar, while with your right hand, the thumb inside, you grip his back collar and adjust your stance as if preparing to apply a chokelock. Then you affix your front chest to your opponent's right back shoulder, pull with both hands with a strangling action, thrust with the upper part of your body and bring your opponent over on to his back.

Method Of Entry By Coiling Right Arm Round Opponent's Neck And Overturning Him:

Although the author does not say so, the context implies that your opponent must be on all-fours or on his stomach. You move round to his head. With your left hand you take hold of his back belt midway and with your right hand, the fingers inside, seize his back collar. Then with both hands you drag and lift him somewhat along the mat. Your right arm is then coiled round your opponent's neck, while with your left hand on his back belt you turn him over to his left side. The upper part of your body, particularly your front chest, is brought to bear heavily down upon your opponent's left chest so that he is pinned on his back for a hold-down.

Method Of Entry By Leg Encirclement And Overturning:

Here again it must be inferred from the context that your opponent is on all-fours or on his stomach. You again move round to his head. With your left hand you take hold of his back belt midway, and with your right hand, fingers inside, you grip his back collar. Pulling and lifting him you pass your right leg from his left side neck stretching and bending it until it reaches his right armpit. Then your left back knee-joint is linked up triangular-wise with your right ankle. Your left hand, removed from your opponent's back belt, is hitched into his left back armpit.

Both hands are now used to confirm control whereupon you fall on your back and capsize your opponent. You turn on to your stomach, get on top of your opponent and essay a hold-down. It is contended that this style of entry affords opportunities for attack by combined Shime and Gyaku and is therefore advantageous.

Method Of Entry By Controlling Opponent's Right Arm With Gyaku And Overturning:

Again, although the author neglects to say so, we must infer from the context that your opponent is on all-fours; otherwise the explanation cannot make sense!

You move round to his right shoulder. Your left hand is thrust from under his left back armpit so as to grip his right front collar, and your right hand is passed from his right side neck under his chin to seize his left side collar. You are thus approximately in a position from which to apply the Okurierijime or Sliding Collar Lock.

Apprehending such an attempt your opponent draws in his chin as a precautionary measure. Now you thrust your left knee into your opponent's right armpit so as to stretch his elbow and bend the elbow-joint to the limit. Your right back heel is then thrust in and stretched and your opponent, not being able to endure the discomfort, extricates his arm whereupon you pin it between your legs, let go your right hand hold of his left side collar, and linking that hand with your left capsize yourself and bring your opponent over on to his back so that you can immobilize him.

This method which provides facilities for application of both Gyaku and Shime is characterized as very advantageous. Thus when you have overturned your opponent and have perhaps failed to immobilize him you may swiftly discard this method, and now from his left side grip his right side lapel with your right hand, the thumb inside, and then hitching your right leg in his left shoulder go for an effective chokelock.

METHODS OF ATTACK BY PULLING IN AND OVERTURNING

Method Of Entry By Utilizing Tomoenage (Stomach Throw):

In this case you are assumed to be engaged in the upright position (Tachiwaza). With your right hand you take hold of your opponent's left outer sleeve midway and with your left hand grasp his right front collar or right sleeve.

You must effect Kuzushi (disturbance of balance) to your opponent's direct front and at the same time let your body slide to the mat under your opponent. You bend your right leg and apply the foot lightly with toes turned back to your opponent's stomach below the navel. The edge of your left ankle is applied to the inner side of his right knee-joint. Then you pull with both hands to reinforce your Kuzushi, straighten your right leg and with your left leg against your opponent's inside knee-joint exert an upward circular movement, as it were, to the left. Then with your right hand holding his left outer sleeve you draw strongly downwards causing him to fall on his back to your right side, whereupon you promptly assume a posture on your stomach preparatory to essaying entry for immobilization.

Method Of Entry By Twisting Opponent's Ankle And Overturning Him:

From the upright stance you take hold of your opponent's left side collar with your left hand, and stooping grip his left ankle with your right hand. Your right foot is planted against his left front waist or lower abdomen. Now as you pull powerfully with your left hand you thrust your right foot against your opponent's body in the manner of the Tomoenage and so hurl him on to his back to your rear, when you may proceed to immobilize him.

Method Of Entry By Reaping Opponent's Leg From Inside:

As you engage your opponent in the upright position you keep on the alert for a moment when his changing posture seems less stable and at once apply your left foot to his left front waist, thrusting strongly, while with your right foot you reap his right leg, upon which he is mostly poised, from the inner side so that as you fall yourself he is thrown to the rear. Without delay you should then get up and from his left side effect your entry for immobilization.

Method Of Entry By Encircling Opponent With Your Legs:

From the upright stance and as you hang on to your opponent with both hands you encircle his torso with both legs and fall backwards. Then with your right hand you seize his left ankle in such wise that you hook his heel, and similarly with your left hand you grip his right ankle again so that you hook his heel. Then you loosen your encircling leg hold on his torso, but pull strongly with both hands gripping his ankles so that deprived of the support of his legs he falls on his back. Instantly availing yourself of the opportunity you get up and sit astride of his stomach to immobilize him.

Method Of Entry By Encircling Opponent's Torso With Your Legs And Gripping His Belt:

With your left hand you grasp your opponent's left side collar and simultaneously with both legs you encircle his torso and as you pull inwards you fall on your back. Drawing strongly with your left hand on his left side collar you effect contact between your left front chest and your opponent's left front chest. Then with your right hand you grip his back belt midway so as to draw it closely towards you.

Letting your right leg slide you hook with it your opponent's right knee-joint; and bending your left leg, with the back of the ankle you hook the inner side of his right thigh, viz. the knee-joint. Concurrently with a downward pull of your right hand holding your opponent's back belt towards your right side, with your right foot you push your opponent's left thigh inwards from the outside and making a circular movement with your left leg you "spring lift" it upwards thereby bringing your opponent on to his back, when you get astride of him to effect immobilization.

Method Of Entry By Overturning Opponent To The Right:

You encircle your opponent with both legs and fall backwards. With your right hand you take hold of his back belt midway, and with your left hand his right rear side belt, and pull him strongly towards you. With your right leg you hook his left leg from the thigh to the knee-joint. Your left back ankle is hitched to his right inner thigh and then assisted with your right leg your left leg is "spring lifted" upwards to the right, and with both your hands you capsize your opponent to the right. It may be that the power of your loins assists this movement more than that of your legs.

Method Of Entry By Hooking Opponent's Outer Left Leg With Your Right Leg:

With your left hand you grip your opponent's left side collar or back collar, your four fingers inside, and with your right hand his left outer sleeve. Your left foot is thrust against his left front waist and your right leg is hitched to his left leg from the outside knee-joint to the ankle.

Although the author fails to say so, it is obvious that with both your legs thus engaged you must fall backwards and indeed this inference is confirmed by the context. You pull strongly with both hands and overturn your opponent to your right side, then get up and effect your entry for immobilization.

Method Of Entry By Controlling Opponent's Right Arm And Overturning Him To Left Side:

Encircling your opponent's torso with both legs you fall backwards. Your right hand is passed over his right shoulder to take hold of his left back belt. Your left hand is inserted under his right front armpit to his back and you draw him closely to your body. Your right back ankle touches his left inner thigh and your left leg envelopes his right leg. With your right leg you "spring lift" your opponent towards your left side. Your left arm passed under your opponent's right front armpit is then manipulated as though to apply an armlock against his right arm. Your right hand passed over his right shoulder and holding his left back belt pulls strongly and this combined action may suffice to overturn him to your left side. Your left leg may also be applied to your opponent's right leg from the knee-joint to the thigh, and then pushed and stretched to facilitate the movement.

Also the power of your right loin rather than that of your right leg may be depended on to consummate this technique. Methods of attack and entry against an opponent attempting immobilization

METHODS OF ATTACK AND ENTRY AGAINST AN OPPONENT ATTEMPTING IMMOBILIZATION

Utilizing Body Tension To Overturn Opponent And Get In:

Your opponent is assumed to be trying to apply a Kuzure-Kesagatame against you, presumably from your right flank. You should endeavour to trap his right arm in your left armpit and with your right arm hug his body closely.

Then bending both legs bring them against his rear loins. Contract your back neck, turn your face to the left. With mobility originating from your legs you should tense your body bow-shape in the sequence chest, left shoulder and head and so contrive to overturn your opponent in the direction of your (left) shoulder, whereupon you must instantly get on your stomach and in your turn endeavour to immobilize your opponent.

Utilizing Body Tension And Twisting Body To Overturn Opponent:

Your opponent is assumed to be applying a Kuzure-Kamishihogatame against you. Contrive to protrude your face and head through his left armpit. Bend both legs and place them at his right side. Your left elbow is stuck against his chest. Your right hand is passed from his right armpit to his back to take hold of his Judogi or your palm is held against the latter. Then as you stretch your body you twist and turn it to the right and overturn your opponent. Then from your stomach you get astride your opponent for immobilization.

Utilizing Body Tension With Your Hand You Overturn Your Opponent And Get In:

Your opponent is applying a Kuzure-Kamishihogatame as before. With your left hand you grasp his back belt midway, and with your right hand his front belt or you affix your hand to his front waist or grip his left or right trouser hem. You bend both legs and make as if to place them at his right side. He will try to resist this movement on your part. Taking advantage of the strength of his resistance and utilizing your body tension you pull and lift with your left hand and push, lift and turn with your right hand so as to capsize your opponent to the left side whereupon you essay to immobilize him.

Utilizing Reaction Or Recoil You Overturn Your Opponent And Get In:

Your opponent is applying a Kuzure-Kesagatame against you. From your waist to your lower limbs you should bring yourself towards your left side and contrive to make a space in the region of his buttocks. Bend and raise both legs. With your right hand grip your opponent's left armpit; stretch your left arm and place it on the mat. Powerfully twist and lower both your raised legs to your left side and simultaneously utilizing the reaction push and let your right hand drop, then as you lift your left elbow raise the upper part of your body, lift your left hand and throw your opponent on his back.

Utilizing Reaction Or Recoil You Overturn Your Opponent:

Again your opponent is applying a Kuzure-Kesagatame against you. Instantly pass your right hand from his right side waist under his armpit and thrust strongly. Then as you stretch your body manoeuvre your opponent in the direction of your head. With your left arm enfold his right arm. With your right hand take hold of his back collar. Bring both your legs to the left and raise them high, and concurrently with the power of the recoil pull and lower strongly with your right hand to capsize your opponent so that you can in your turn get in for immobilization.

Method Of Entry By Getting Up From Direction Of Opponent's Buttocks And Overturning Him:

In this case your opponent is applying the Hongesagatame as usual from the right. With your left hand grasp his back belt midway or push strongly in the region of his right back shoulder. Bring yourself from the waist downwards to your left, your face turned to the right. As you extricate (if possible!) your right arm from your opponent's left armpit and if from your waist downwards you can get on to your stomach, then gradually assume a squatting posture and create a gap in the direction of your opponent's buttocks he may spontaneously fall on to his back.

This method of countering is one much practised by persons of a soft and pliant habit of body and is therefore very suitable for young Judoka.

Method Of Entry By Overturning Opponent To Left Side:

Your opponent is attacking you with a Kuzure-Kesagatame. With your left arm you trap his right arm and simultaneously with that hand firmly grip his left back belt. Your right hand palm is pressed against the area of your opponent's body from his right front waist to his abdominal region. You bend both your legs and bring them to your right flank and with your left hand which holds your opponent's left back belt you draw downwards to the left side as with your right hand you impart a pushing lifting movement and utilizing your body tension overturn your opponent to your left side so that you can in your turn try to immobilize him.

Method Of Entry By Controlling Opponent's Hand With Belt And Overturning Him:

When having encircled your opponent's torso with both legs you fall backwards, and should he stretch out his left hand, with your right hand you clutch his wrist and make as if to attempt the Hantai-Udegarami against that arm. In order to ward off the attack your opponent may grip your left side belt (with his left hand). In that case you thrust your left hand from under his left back armpit and effect contact between the back of your wrist and his left wrist. With your right hand you take hold of your belt a little to the left of where he is gripping it with his left hand. Then if you pull strongly and transfer your hold to your left hand his left hand grasping your left side belt should be perfectly controlled whereupon you at once unloosen your leg hold on his torso, turn him over either to the left or rear and essay immobilization.

Method Of Entry By Utilizing Hantai-Udegarami And Overturning Opponent:

You have encircled your opponent's body with both legs and have fallen backwards. If he stretches out his left arm then with your right hand you grasp his left wrist, raise the upper part of your body and thrust your left arm deeply from his left back armpit as though, as in the former instance, contemplating a Hantai-Udegarami. If the Gyaku is efficacious he may move to your left side and fall on his back. In this case it is possible that the encounter will terminate in a Gyaku instead of a pure immobilization.

Taking Advantage Of Withdrawal Of Opponent's Right Leg To Overturn Him And Get In:

In this case it is assumed that you are underneath your opponent and are defending yourself in either A-style or B-style.

If in A-style you are gripping his left lapel with your left hand and his left ankle or bottom of his trousers with your right hand. Your right foot is planted against his left front waist and as you pull strongly with both hands you thrust forcibly with your right foot. Your left foot is planted against his right front chest or front waist or is hitched into his right knee-joint.

If in B-style your right leg is passed from the inside of his front thigh so that from the knee-joint you hook it from above. Then you hook the back part of your left knee-joint into his right ankle and your left ankle is linked from below his right ankle with the toes bent and stretched backwards so that his right leg is clipped, stretched out and with difficulty able to extricate itself. If, however, he manages to withdraw it and tries to apply an Osaekomi method, then with your left hand passed from his left shoulder you take hold of his back belt, and with your right hand the bottom of his trousers or the inside of the knee-joint. You bend both legs and bring them to the right. With your left hand you endeavour to pull and lift your opponent. You stretch your body. With your right hand you push, lift and turn your opponent in the direction of your head and overturn him to the left side. Your right hand may also be inserted between your opponent's thighs to grip his back belt or simply inserted to assist the overturning movement.

This counter is vulgarly known as Teppogaeshi, literally "gun-counter".

Utilizing Withdrawal Of Opponent's Leg To Overturn Him To Left Side:
Again you are supposed to be underneath your opponent and defending yourself in B-style previously described. If your opponent tries to extricate his leg (?the right), then you pass your right hand over his right shoulder and grasp his back belt, pulling strongly with that hand. With your left hand passed from under his right armpit you enfold his forearm. To prevent the withdrawal of your opponent's right leg you may exert yourself to the utmost in invoking the C-style defence in which you hook your opponent's leg from the outside with your left leg, the toes bent backwards. Your right leg is passed from the inside of his right front thigh so that the rear side of the knee-joint links up with your left ankle. Your right ankle passes from under his right ankle, toes bent backwards, and stretches his right ankle so that he cannot easily extricate it. You raise the upper part of your body and apply your right ankle to his left inner knee-joint. Then as with both legs you "spring-lift", pull strongly, lift and drop with your right hand and overturn your opponent to the direct rear or right back corner. This is also a very important method capable of application either when your opponent is standing or in a half-sitting position on the mat.

Utilizing Withdrawal Of Opponent's Leg To Overturn Him:
You have fallen on your back and from underneath your opponent are resorting to the B-style and C-style, already described, to entangle his legs.

Your right hand is passed from your opponent's right shoulder to take hold of his back belt, and you pull strongly with that hand. If your opponent finds it hard to extricate his right leg he may make a move to effect an immobilization hold. He may bring back his hips to the left and while making desperate efforts to extricate his right leg wheel round in the direction of your head.

Now with your right hand on his back belt continue to pull strongly while you more and more try to turn your opponent in the direction of your head. The back of your right leg is applied to his left inner thigh. With your left hand you clasp his right thigh. Your left instep is applied to the inside of his right thigh. If you twist your body to the right as though to get up and adapt the natural change of your posture to the strength of your opponent's efforts to immobilize you, he may fall on his back to the left side. Keeping pace with him you should get astride without delay to immobilize him in your turn.

Method Of Entry By Overturning In Direction Of Head:
When your opponent is attacking you with a Katagatame (Shoulder Lock) and both your arms are being held in contact, you push strongly against his right side neck, inhale deeply, contract your back neck, turn your face to your right side, lift both legs as high as possible oscillating them violently. Utilize the recoil and turn yourself over in the direction of your left shoulder.

Extricate your head from under your opponent's right armpit. Contrive to trap his right arm in your right armpit so that it is menaced with Gyaku to elude which he may turn himself over to the front. In that case without delaying an instant get astride the upper part of his body, chest or stomach and attempt immobilization in your turn.

Method Of Entry By Controlling Opponent's Elbow:
You have fallen on your back. Your opponent using his left leg to bestride your right thigh mounts your torso. With his right hand he clasps your left hip and assumes a posture intimating that he contemplates immobilization tactics. Using both legs you have recourse to the B-style and C-style of

defence already explained in detail, so as to foil your opponent's efforts to extricate his right leg.

You grip his wrist (which one not stated) with your right hand, and your left hand is applied to his front shoulder from his left side neck. Your opponent tries to defend himself against your approach in the direction of his head and gradually advances from your left shoulder when with your right hand passed from his lower arm over his left shoulder you grip your own right front collar so that his left elbow is controlled triangular-wise. Your left hand grips his back belt midway. You now relinquish your leg entanglement of your opponent's legs and bring both your legs to the right side. Pulling and lifting with your left hand you stretch your body and twisting and turning your opponent from the direction of your head capsize him.

In this case, too, you may be able to help the process of capsizing your opponent by "spring lifting" him with the instep of your left foot applied to his right leg from underneath.

The foregoing somewhat abbreviated selection of Hairikata or methods of entry completes the exposition of Osaekomiwaza based on Oda's system and I leave it to be gradually assimilated by the patient reader!

CHAPTER V
INTRODUCTION TO SHIMEWAZA OR NECKLOCKS—BASIC PRINCIPLES

WITH much of the matter contained in Oda's introduction most Judoka or at any rate Yudansha are already familiar. They are, for instance, generally aware that the objectives of attack by means of necklocks are the carotid arteries, the jugular veins (the external jugular more particularly) and the trachea or windpipe in varying degrees. And in this connexion a fact perhaps not so generally known is that the right carotid artery (right side of neck) is more vulnerable to strangulation than the left—a detail which can advantageously be borne in mind when one is bent upon most expeditiously reducing one's victim to submission by the shortest route!

For those of my readers that are anxious in all cases to master the relevant Judo terminology—as all zealous Judoka ought to be—I may add that when inadvertently the victim of a necklock loses consciousness through failure to give the signal of defeat in time he is said to have "ochiita" (literally, "fallen", from the verb "ochiiru" meaning to fall, drop, collapse, etc.). And as doubtless most of you already know, the accepted method of signaling defeat when one is deprived of speech is to tap twice smartly with hand or foot one's opponent's body or the mat. Once the victim loses consciousness an effective method of Katsu or resuscitation must promptly be applied by the referee or other competent Yudansha whether during formal contest (Shobu or Shiai) or Randori (free practice). Oda takes care to deprecate obstinate refusal to surrender and thus to incur the risk of syncope rather than admit defeat which reflects no disgrace whatever upon any contestant.

The circumstances in which necklocks can be applied are truly legion. They include the standing position, underneath one's opponent, on top of him, from the rear, the side, etc., etc. And openings are afforded in the course of Nagewaza, Osaekomiwaza and Kansetsuwaza, so that as a means to the speediest development of Shimewaza none of these branches of the art should be neglected. Moreover, as will later be seen and as indeed I have already intimated, nearly all such examples involve the use of one or both legs to supplement the inferior power of the hands, in gratifying contradistinction to the previous practice which banned that expedient to the no little detriment of an art which must, however volubly the unduly squeamish may try to deny the obvious, ever remain *sui generis* a fighting art, whatever else it may be.

Thus the erstwhile official refusal to countenance the application of legs and thighs to the victim's neck and throat and to teach the most effective methods of using the lower extremities for strangulation purposes has hitherto potentially imposed a fatuous handicap upon Judoka in the event of their being engaged in a genuine struggle for survival.

As a "major premise" it may safely be postulated that an attack from your opponent's rear has much to recommend it. One of the simplest "gambits" is thus described: Its immediate object is not so much the actual application of a necklock as the creation of an opening for that purpose.

Pass your left hand under your opponent's left rear armpit and take hold of his front collar and similarly pass your right hand under his right rear armpit so as to grip his right front collar or lapel from the front downwards. Although the author does not here specify the form of hand-hold or Kumikata, actual experience will suffice to show that the hold implied must be the reverse of Gyaku grip with the four fingers inside and the thumb outside the lapel. Then while hanging on to his body encircle him with your legs from about the outside of his thighs and let yourself fall to your direct back or else with your left leg hooking your opponent's left leg from back to front throw yourself not so much to your direct back as obliquely in a left lateral direction. It is theoretically assumed that in this position your opponent will become more or less vulnerable to a selected necklock.

Again, it may happen that dreading your Nagewaza your opponent will seek to force a draw by placing one knee on the mat or even by taking up a posture on all-fours. In that case, approaching from behind him, with your right hand passing from his right collar grip his back collar with your four fingers inside, i.e. the Gyaku hold, retreat a step with your right leg in such wise as to force his forehead to the mat causing him as it were to slump towards his left front corner on all-fours or on his stomach. Then instantly mount him from the rear, horseback fashion and apply one or other of the necklocks already described.

Another hypothetical case. Assuming that with your legs encircling your opponent's torso or else both his legs (from the front) you have fallen on your back.

With your left hand, the four fingers inside, you are grasping his left side collar and have set as your ultimate objective sooner or later the application of a necklock from his rear or are maneuvering positively to that end. Your opponent on his part is perhaps planning recourse to Osaekomi or immobilization. With your left foot applied to his front waist or above his thigh you defend yourself against his efforts to find an opening. Now with your right foot hook the outer side of his left leg while you draw your left hand (which is gripping his left side collar) in the direction of your left shoulder and with your right hand take hold of his left side belt. In this position with your right leg you thrust powerfully towards the upper part of your opponent's right thigh from the back of his left rear thigh. If this manoeuvre succeeds he should revolve so that he falls with his back to your front when you at once entwine your legs round his torso and resort to an effective combination stranglehold from behind.

The gist of this introductory matter is that you must strive to achieve a technique that will enable you to control your opponent's bodily movements from almost every position. Among the essential manoeuvres for this purpose it will be clear that leg encirclement of your opponent's trunk plays a highly important role, as also the ability to hamper his movements with your feet against his front waist, if he is bending or lying over you, e.g. in an attempt to find an opening on his own part for a necklock or a hold-down. At this stage the author interpolates his seven alphabetical categories from A-style to G-style which may be said briefly to embody certain basic principles, on the natural assumption that the intelligent student will know how empirically to apply these categories and basic principles to a given situation. Here then are these seven categories.

A-style: Turn to your opponent's back and mount him horseback fashion. It must be assumed that he is already on all-fours. Pass your left hand under his left rear armpit and with the four fingers inside grip his left front collar. Pass your right hand under his right rear armpit and similarly grip his right front collar. With your left leg hook your opponent's left leg by thrusting it against his inner thigh, and similarly entangle his right leg with your right leg pressing against his inner thigh. If from this position you bring all your weight to bear in a forward direction you ought to be able to control his body.

B-style: Attack from the rear. Take hold of your opponent's left and right front collars as described in A-style above. Encircle his trunk with both legs so as to bring their insteps into close contact. In this position you should be able to control his freedom of action.

C-style: Again attack from the rear. Grip your opponent's left and right front collars as described in A-style. Your right leg passed from behind your opponent should be brought into contact with the lower part of his abdomen, with your knee-joint and under touching his belt. Your left knee-joint hooks your right ankle. The tip of your left foot hooking your right ankle presses strongly against your opponent's rear loin and in this manner you control his freedom of movement.

D-style: Although the author omits to say so, for a proper understanding of this movement you must presuppose that your opponent is lying on his back and that you are about to attack him seated from behind. Now pass your *right* leg across the *left* side of his neck and over his breast as far as his *right* armpit. Then thrust your *left* leg underneath his back until the under curve of the knee-joint links up with your *right* ankle. Your *left* hand should be inserted under your opponent's left armpit and freely utilized to help in immobilizing his left arm and generally in controlling his freedom of movement. Remember again that these alphabetical styles are not intended to be an exposition of actual necklocks but rather, as already emphasized, "gambits" calculated to provide convenient openings for recourse to strangleholds and choking methods.

E-style: Again it must be assumed that your opponent is lying on his back and that you are preparing to attack from behind from a recumbent position. Always assuming that your opponent has inadvertently somewhat extended his *right* arm, bring your *right* leg heavily to bear down upon his *right* forearm while your *left* leg is thrust under his *right* armpit from behind so that from both thighs downwards to the tips of your feet you can hold his entire right arm in a crushing scissor-like grip. Then your *left* hand is, as before, inserted through his left back armpit and manipulated so as to hamper his freedom of movement.

F-style: Less elaborate. You are supposed to be lying on your back with your legs encircling your opponent's trunk as he bends over you. Your legs are then manipulated to hamper his freedom of movement.

G-style: Again you are lying on your back with your opponent on top and you use your hands to hold his lapels while your feet against his front waist are thrust and stretched so as to hamper his freedom of movement.

In further illustration of the application of these categories the writer cites a few more hypothetical instances.

Assuming again a projected attack from your opponent's rear, in the expectation of your attempted necklock your opponent may devise various defensive expedients. Let us assume then that he is in a semi-recumbent, semi-sitting posture, on all-fours or on his stomach. From behind him with your right hand, thumb inside, take hold of his right side collar and using the full strength of that arm with the weight of your body behind it thrust your hand under his chin, holding yourself simultaneously in readiness to counter his defensive measures and to take advantage of the first opportunity to effect an entry. The thrusting force of your right hand should in this position be considerable. Eventually it may prove too much for your opponent's powers of resistance and result in the momentary exposure of his throat. It will then be up to you to break through his defences and apply your chosen necklock.

In the next hypothetical case it is assumed that you are controlling your opponent's torso in A-style, i.e. mounted on his back and facing the same way. Thrust your left hand under his left armpit, catch his left wrist with that hand and pull it backwards. Your right hand may then be made into a fist and with the full weight of your body behind it thrust under your opponent's throat. Alternatively the open hand may be used for this purpose. The author states that the method of thrusting with the closed hand, thumb inside, was at one time called the "tank" or "tanku" and gained great popularity. The practice of attacking with the "tank" method from both sides of the victim's neck was continued for some time.

Finally one more example of the A-style approach mounted on your opponent's back and in that position controlling his body. Pass your left hand under his left back armpit, catch his left wrist and draw it backwards. Your *right* hand is passed from his *left* side neck to his forehead so that your *right* elbow is parallel with the mat. Then while pushing to the right from the left twist your right hand to the rear so as to contain your opponent's head and expose his throat; then pulling out your left hand pass it from the direction of your opponent's left back side neck under his throat until it reaches and grips his right front and side collar in order to apply a decisive necklock.

Before passing on in the next chapter to a detailed exposition of the Oda Shimewaza repertoire I consider it advisable to cite briefly four cardinal tenets or principles applicable to Shimewaza generally, viz.

(1) It is essential in all cases to secure control of your opponent's freedom of movement.

(2) On no account should your strangling and choking arm be used like a hard unyielding stick or pole but rather as though it were a thick clinging rope capable of closely constricting your opponent's neck and throat and merging, so to speak, into all their crannies and interstices.

(3) You must always strive to preserve conditions enabling you to move your own body to the fullest extent required for application of the chosen method.

(4) When applying a necklock use only the minimum portion of your arm necessary to produce the required effect.

In this context it is well to remember that a trained Judoka's neck is generally pretty strong so that unless you can control his freedom of movement your Shimewaza is not likely to prove efficacious. Your opponent may be afforded an opportunity to bring about a situation in which he can easily alter his position. If, for example, he manages to get on to his feet he may detect an opening in his turn for the application of a standing necklock and in this manner you may incur the risk of being exposed to a devastating counter-attack or Gyakugeki.

Again, if you apply your necklock with your arm held stiffly, stick-wise, the most vulnerable part of his neck and throat may conceivably escape and thus the effect of your necklock will be nullified. That is why your arm should be used rather as a soft rope so that it can be twined or coiled round the actual vulnerable portion of your opponent's neck and throat. Also the efficacy of a necklock tends to be impaired if the strength of your acting arm is dissipated beyond the actual vulnerable area. You should therefore train yourself assiduously in order to be able in a flash to assume the most suitable posture for a decisive Shime attack.

It must further be borne in mind that if when attempting to strangle your opponent you fail to achieve conditions conducive to your own free movement not only will you be unable to control your opponent but the physical strength or vital force passing from your body into your hands and arms will not suffice to ensure success.

A final caution is necessary. While ruthless Shime methods necessitating the application of one or both legs are deliberately included in the Oda repertoire dealt with in the next chapter and may with due care be tested in Keiko or practice, they are still strictly prohibited in contest or Shiai. This embargo extends to the so-called Dojime or trunk-squeezing described in my *Manual of Judo*, but not included in the Oda repertoire. The reason for their exclusion is that they are considered to be too dangerous for use in friendly competition when perhaps in the excitement of the moment a victorious contestant may inflict serious damage upon his victim before the referee has time to call a halt.

CHAPTER VI
EXPOSITION OF SHIMEWAZA

IN the Oda version of Shimewaza no attempt is made to adhere to the generally adopted sequence in which the so-called Namijujijime or Normal Cross is usually first described. Oda omits this technique altogether and gives precedence to the Hadakajime or Naked Chokelock. Thus:

HADAKAJIME
(NAKED CHOKELOCK)

From a practical standpoint this method of strangulation is one of the most formidable in the copious Shimewaza repertoire. Unlike most necklocks the Hadakajime is not dependent upon the victim's collar and lapels for its successful execution but can be freely resorted to against a naked adversary. Although this method can be utilized against an opponent in various positions, e.g. while he is standing, falling backwards, stooping, etc., perhaps the most opportune moment is when he is seated on the mat with legs crossed or partly so, in tailor fashion called in Japanese, *agura wo kaku*. In that case you approach him from the rear, one knee on the mat and the other raised and bent.

In his text the author describes the *left* knee as being on the mat whereas the attached Fig. 29 shows the assailant as posed with his *right* knee on the mat! Analogous discrepancies not infrequently occur throughout the text and have to be rectified. Your right arm is passed from over your opponent's right shoulder so that approximately the middle part of the forearm is applied to the front of his throat and bent to the left. It is essential that the *thumb edge* of your right forearm should be kept in contact with your opponent's throat, specifically against his trachea or windpipe. Your left arm is passed from over your opponent's left shoulder and your right hand, palm downwards, is placed in the crook of your left elbow while the palm of your left hand presses firmly against your opponent's occiput. Then as you withdraw your body somewhat to the rear you pull and lift with your right forearm constricting your opponent's throat from the front and coordinate this action with the propulsion of your left hand against his occiput, so that his body is tilted backwards about 45 degrees, his windpipe is, as it were, crushed between the two opposing forces and his respiration is cut off. The illustration also indicates that your right cheek is pressed against the left side of your opponent's head and that your right front shoulder is pushed against his back neck (Fig. 29).

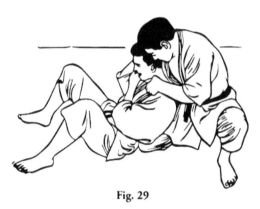

Fig. 29

In an alternative method, not illustrated but easily understood, instead of placing your right palm in the crook of your left elbow-joint, you cup it downwards in the upheld palm of your left hand which rests upon your opponent's left shoulder. Then your right shoulder is pressed against his occiput and the right side of your head against the back of his head, and as before you draw his body backwards in the synchronized action of constricting his windpipe between the backward tension of your right arm and the forward pressure of your right shoulder and head. On the whole, however, the first method seems likely to be the more effective of the two.

It ought not to be necessary to point out that the Hadakajime can just as easily, in the case of a left-handed Judoka, be applied in the opposite direction. This means that your *left* forearm is passed from over your opponent's left shoulder across his throat, with the palm cushioned in the crook of your *right* elbow-joint; that the palm of your right hand is pressed against your opponent's occiput, and that your left cheek is held against the right side of your opponent's head. The remaining movements are virtually the same as in the orthodox right-arm method.

It seems a pity that Oda should have omitted a description of yet another method of executing the Hadakajime which I have included in my *Manual of Judo* and which is, in my opinion, the simplest and far and away the most effective of any. On the assumption that the tensile strength of one's right hand and arm is usually greater than that of one's left, this method can perhaps be best applied by using your left forearm to constrict your seated opponent's throat from behind with your right knee on the mat. Or alternatively you can attack standing up with your left knee pressed against your opponent's spine and your right leg stretched to the rear, and indeed this method has much to recommend it.

Take care as before that the *thumb edge* of your left forearm is applied to your opponent's windpipe. Cup the downward palm of your left hand crosswise in the upheld palm of your right hand the back of which is slightly above your opponent's right shoulder but remains free to manipulate as occasion may require. With the left side of your head push strongly to the left against the right side of your opponent's head and synchronize this action with the sustained pressure of your left forearm against his windpipe and the maximum backward tension of your right hand gripping your left in the region of your opponent's right shoulder. When all is said and done the acid test in Judo should be the empiric and not the "bookish theoric", and if subjected to that test I am inclined to think that this last named method will gain most suffrages.

OKURIERIJIME
(SLIDING COLLAR LOCK)

The author explains two methods, viz. "A" and "B". In his first method "A" he presupposes that you are attacking from your opponent's rear and have brought him on to his back over you in such wise that your legs are encircling him with the insteps in contact or the feet simply crossed above his hips. Your right hand is passed over his right back shoulder under his throat to grip his left side collar with the thumb inside; your left hand is passed under his left back armpit to grip his right front collar or side collar also with the thumb inside. Inhale deeply and simultaneously tug powerfully with both hands on your opponent's lapels as it were in the direction of your left and right side chest. Curve your body and force back your opponent's body to form an arc and in this manner consummate the necklock.

Points to be observed are that your forehead can advantageously be pressed against the nape of your opponent's neck or else you may hold your right cheek in contact with his left cheek. For the successful application of this chokelock you must train yourself in the coordinated use of both hands and legs and be ever on the alert not to expose your legs encircling your opponent's body to entanglement through leg manoeuvres on his part. He might, for example, hook your right or left ankle with his right or left back ankle and then catch and stretch the knee-joint of the captured leg from underneath in such a way that your ankle would be trapped and unable to slip out, so that an unwary movement might injure it. Thus it might then be difficult for you to curve your body when trying the chokelock with both hands. You are therefore urged to be careful when encircling your opponent with your legs in order to avoid this danger.

Another example of the use of the legs in the Okurierijime is given as follows:

Remember that your opponent is assumed to be lying on his back as before and that you are attacking on your back from underneath his body. Effect adequate control of your opponent's body by using your right leg twined so as to bring it from his right rear to his front waist or lower abdomen, the rear side of the leg from the knee-joint downwards being more or less parallel with his belt; your left knee-joint is linked with the back of your right ankle, and your left ankle is thrust hard against your opponent's left (sic) rear thigh or waist to complete control of his counter movements.

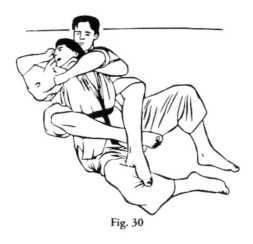

Fig. 30

The author has clearly here been guilty of a slip in his description since it would be physically impossible for you to thrust your left ankle against your opponent's left rear thigh if your left knee-joint were already linked with the back of your own right ankle. Therefore for "left rear thigh" We must surely read "right inner thigh". This type of hold is especially suitable for a man with long legs and once it has been applied it will usually prove very difficult for the victim to escape. But of course it is imperative that you should be equally solicitous to achieve dexterity in the coordinated use of your hands to ensure the success of this method.

In his efforts to thwart your application of the Okurierijime your opponent may with both hands grip your right side collar or right upper sleeve and pull hard on it, and bending his legs, stretching and bending his body bow-fashion strive to avert strangulation. In that case loosen the hold of both your legs encircling his torso, bring them to the upper side and exerting yourself to deflect your opponent towards his right or left side hook him with your right leg from the knee-joint to the ankle from above his hands which are pulling your right side collar or upper sleeve towards his right shoulder or left breast; link your left back ankle with your right ankle, and as with both hands you exert the maximum tension on your opponent's throat, tense your body, stretch both legs and as his right hand loses its hold on your right side collar or upper sleeve consummate the choking process. Or even if his hand hold is not relaxed you may be able to choke him effectively.

Another variant: Unloosen your linked feet entwined round your opponent's torso, and bring them to the upper side. Catch his left wrist with your left hand, snatch it away and stretch it backwards; pass your right knee-joint across his right chest from over his right wrist so that the underside comes in contact with it; the rear side of that ankle touches his right (sic ?left) armpit; your right leg engages the region of his chest and stomach from the back to the right side. Then as you choke him with both hands push and stretch your right leg when your opponent's right hand may spontaneously loosen its hold on your collar and so facilitate the application of the chokelock.

Again, your opponent controlled by your legs encircling his trunk from the rear may try to protect himself by grasping his front or side collar and drawing in his chin. In that case bring your left leg in contact with the right side of his chest and stomach; with your right foot hook him from his right shoulder; thrust and stretch the back heel of that foot against the outer side of his bent elbow-joint; pluck away his right hand, crush his right arm between both legs and complete the chokelock as before.

Next, your opponent fearing your chokelock may intersect your hands and grip his right or left front collar (or side collar), draw in his chin as far as possible to his chest and offer a strong resistance. As before, attacking from his rear encircle his torso with your legs, turn your right hand over your opponent's defending hands from the right back and grip his left front collar; pass your left hand under his left back armpit and grasp is right front collar with the thumb inside; stretch both legs, bend your own body and your opponent's bow fashion, and with the maximum traction of both your hands choke him. Supposing that the chokelock should at first prove abortive, then unloosen your legs, catch your opponent's left hand with your left hand; twist yourself to the right side, lower your body, make as if to go for a hold-down when your opponent may relinquish his right-hand hold and so inadvertently expose his threat to attack, not necessarily with the Okurierijime but perhaps with the Katahajime (Single Wing Lock) or even with the Kuzure-Kamishihogatame or Broken Locking of the Four Quarters.

OKURIERIJIME
(SLIDING COLLAR LOCK) B

It is assumed in this case that your opponent is in a half-sitting, half-rising posture, on all-fours or on his stomach. Approach from his true right side, viewed from behind him, so that you are bending over the back of his prostrate head more or less at right-angles. Now pass your *right hand* from the direction of his right rear and side neck under his throat and clutch his *left side collar* with the thumb inside; pass your *left hand* from under his left back armpit to grip his *right side collar* also with the thumb inside. Your body is bearing down heavily upon your opponent's head and occiput and his back neck touches the region of your left front waist. Stretch out your left leg and plant your right foot on the mat with the knee bent. Push strongly against your opponent's back neck with your left front waist; draw your right elbow towards your right front chest and your left elbow towards your left side chest, and with both hands choke your opponent for all you are worth (Fig. 31).

Fig. 31

KATAJUJIJIME
(HALF CROSS LOCK)

There are two generally recognized methods of executing this effective necklock, viz.

(1) from a position astride your opponent's body and

(2) from the side of your opponent who has fallen sideways.

Our author's method differs appreciably from both of these and it therefore seems advisable for purposes of comparison to preface his pet Katajujijime with a succinct explanation of the first two.

In the first instance having assumed the equestrian or astride position on your opponent's torso which should be firmly held between both your knees and feet so that you can control his freedom of movement, with your left hand you take hold of your opponent's left back collar in the reverse or *Gyaku* grip, i.e. fingers inside, and with your right hand passed over your left arm take a deep hold of his right side collar in the regular or *Jun-ni* grip. As regards your left hand grip be careful that the bend of your thumb presses against your opponent's left carotid artery, and that the little finger edge of your right hand and arm constricts his neck from his right carotid artery to his windpipe.

To effect the actual chokelock with both hands, you pull powerfully with your left hand gripping his left back collar and push with your right hand holding his right side collar and bend your body forward. Should it happen that you are tackling an exceptionally stout adversary and you try to control his torso with your knees and feet, you run the risk of being capsized from your astride position. To avert this danger you are advised to keep one knee raised with your foot on the mat.

It is not necessary that your left hand hold on your adversary's left back collar should be very deep because if it is, seeing that the action of both your hands is correlated, the freedom of movement of your right hand tends to be restricted, and in this way the efficacy of the necklock is weakened. You should therefore try to preserve a position enabling you to manipulate your right hand and arm freely between: your opponent's chin and your own left arm. On the other hand if your grip is too shallow the necklock is likely to fail. At the crucial moment you must seek to control your opponent's trunk between your knees and feet so that he cannot shift to right or left; otherwise he may succeed in twisting his body and getting up.

As regards the second method, this is attempted from the Tachiwaza position and opportunities for its execution are not infrequent. If, for example, your opponent has fallen sideways and you attack him from his left side, grip his left side collar with your left hand, fingers inside, and his right collar with your right hand, the thumb inside, and as you hamper his freedom of action with your left knee against his torso endeavour to choke him into submission.

Now for the Oda method. From the standing position you first pass your left hand from your opponent's left side collar to his back collar which you grip with the four fingers inside (the reverse or Gyaku hold) and then fall back dragging him over you. Then you pass your right hand over your left arm from your opponent's right side collar to his back collar which you grip with the thumb inside (the normal hold). Both your feet are applied to your opponent's front waist and pushed strongly against it, thus breaking his balance to the front (*mamae-no-kuzushi*); you then twist your right wrist strongly from left to right so as to bring the maximum pressure to bear against his right carotid artery. Now inhale deeply, and as you raise your lower abdomen from your front waist exert the force of both your hands to choke your opponent into submission (Fig. 32).

Fig. 32

NARABIJUJIJIME
(ALIGNED CROSS CHOKELOCK)

When your opponent is lying on his back an opening may be afforded for recourse to this method. Get astride his torso with both your legs gripping it so that you can control his movements. Pass your right hand across his right side collar to his back collar and grip the latter with your thumb inside, palm downwards, otherwise the normal hold, and pass your left hand under your right hand and forearm and across your opponent's left side collar to his back collar which you grasp with the same hold. Incline the upper part of your body forward concentrating its weight upon both your wrists. Exert the maximum tightening tension with both hands so as to choke your victim into submission (Fig. 33).

Fig. 33

It may be remarked that in some respects this particular necklock resembles the more familiar Namijujijime or Normal Cross in which the attacker's hands grip the victim's lapels in much the same way. However, in the Narabijujijime you take a grip appreciably farther behind your opponent's neck than in the Namijujijime. Then, too, the author supplements his basic description with a series of variants involving alternative or modified action of your arms and legs designed to impart the maximum efficacy to the Aligned Cross Necklock. These additional hints may be summarized as follows:

Method Of Gripping The Collar:
(1) If you first grip your opponent's left side collar with your left hand then your right hand should pass over that hand to grip his right side collar.

(2) It is also possible, when holding your opponent's left side collar with your left hand, to pass your right hand from his left side collar behind his head so as to grip his right side collar, when in applying the actual chokelock you twine the collar tightly round from the direction of his (right) back neck in conjunction with the tension of your left hand gripping his left side or left back collar.

(3) When you are grasping your opponent's left side collar with your left hand you can also with your right hand take hold of his jacket near his right back shoulder.

Use Of Legs:
With both legs confining your opponent's trunk you apply tightening pressure to his front waist.

Method Of Using Hands:
(1) Practise drawing back both hands with maximum power when choking opponent.

(2) Similarly practise pressing them forward for the same purpose or in anatomical parlance uniformly exercise both your abductor and adductor muscles.

Method Of Exposing Opponent's Neck And Throat To Attack:
When you are looking for an opening to apply a necklock against an opponent lying on his back, as often as not he will try to defend himself by drawing in his chin. And in such cases the rules of contest forbid the reckless pressure of your forearm against his chin, teeth or lips and should the referee detect recourse to such tactics on the part of any contestant it is his duty at once to intervene. It must therefore be your object to achieve victory by strict adherence to the rules.

Let us then assume that with both hands you have taken what seems to be a suitable hold of your opponent's collar. Now with an eye on your objective suddenly and powerfully raise them somewhat when the impetus of this movement coupled with the force of gravity may cause your opponent's head to fall back thus exposing his throat and neck to your assault. Then without delay insert your wrists for the application of your projected method, e.g. the Reverse Cross Necklock or Gyakujujijime, the Half Cross Necklock or Katajujijime, etc., etc.

In this connexion, let us say that your opponent is lying with his left side towards you and that you are contemplating a necklock, it is important not to forget to use your left leg so as to keep down his right front waist. And perhaps most important of all is the sedulous cultivation of the grasping power of both your arms by means of systematic bending and flexing practice to impart suppleness to the elbow joints. And all instructors should encourage beginners to carry out these exercises as an integral part of their training. Neglect to take a sufficiently deep hold of your opponent's collar may easily represent all the difference between success and failure in your execution of the projected necklock.

KUBIJIME
(NECK CHOKE)

This necklock is applied to an opponent on all-fours and you are in front of him with your right knee on the mat. You pass your right hand from over his left rear so as to encircle his side neck, while with your left hand you grip your own right wrist from under his right neck and throat. Then with your chest you press down heavily against the back of your opponent's head (the occiput); combine this movement with a twist somewhat to the right and a lift with your right wrist against his throat thereby choking him into submission in a vice-like grip (Fig. 34).

Fig. 34

Alternative hand-holds against your opponent's throat which seem in some ways preferable to the foregoing are:

(1) to join your two palms in such wise that your left hand palm is cupped, so to speak, in the palm of your right hand, with the four fingers overlapping and

(2) to unite both hands in such a way that the nails dig into the base of the fingers of both hands, the palm of your left hand uppermost, while the thumb edge of your right wrist cuts into your opponent's throat. This last-named style of clutch is familiar to all catch-as-catch-can wrestlers who invariably employ it when applying a half or three-quarter nelson to a kneeling opponent's neck. On no account must your fingers be interlaced because in that form of grip they cannot be unloosened and extricated quickly enough in an emergency, e.g. when changing position.

In another variant you can encircle your opponent's body with your legs and fall upon your back.

Also if your opponent is in a half-sitting half-rising posture and clings to your waist or legs, you may attempt to apply this lock from a standing position.

ERIJIME
(COLLAR OR LAPEL CHOKE)

This necklock is first applied when you are engaged with your opponent in Tachiwaza or a standing position. With your right hand grip your opponent's left side collar in the normal hold, the thumb inside, and with your left hand take a similar hold of his right side collar. Endeavour to draw his forehead downwards towards your chest; combine the side grip with both hands on both sides of your opponent's neck with a drawing lifting movement which will crush his carotid arteries and cut off his respiration (Fig. 35).

Fig. 35

As in other locks already described, this method can be converted into a recumbent attack as you fall on your back and encircle your opponent's trunk with your legs. If he is in a half-sitting half-rising posture, you can thrust and stretch both feet against his front waist and so help to immobilize him. Lying on your back bring the inside of your right thigh over your right fist and your left thigh over your left fist and in contact with them; then from above your hands gripping your opponent's neck on either side, as you raise them suddenly crush his carotid artery between both inner thighs which are in contact with your thumbs. It may again be worthwhile to point out that this drastic use of the legs to reinforce hand holds is forbidden in contest and would not formerly have been allowed even in Randori. But *"tempora mutantur, nos et mutamur in illis"*, and a very good thing too in the domain of Judo which must on no account be permitted to become static in a groove and thereby forfeit its dynamic attributes.

TSUKKOMIJIME
(THRUSTING CHOKELOCK)

Your opponent is lying on his back and you are astride of him in good control of his torso. With your left hand grasp his right side collar in the normal hold, the thumb inside, and with your right hand take a reverse grip (four fingers inside lapel), low down on your opponent's left front lapel; then raise and draw it tightly across his throat towards his right side neck and by means of the combined thrusting pressure of both hands choke him into submission.

Among several other minor modifications of hold described, the author explains a variant in which with your left hand you grip *both* your opponent's lapels and with your right hand similarly grip both lapels *below* your left hand. Then you are told to combine a twisting thrusting pressure of your *right* hand with the sustained traction of your *left* hand. I have the nerve to suggest that a far more effective way of using this dual lapel hold is to reverse the order, i.e. with your left upper hand grip you should *thrust upwards* into your opponent's windpipe and exert your lower right hand hold to impart the necessary traction.

Incidentally the latter method was well known and practised in virtually every Jujutsu Ryugi Dojo long before the foundation of the Kodokan. It was indeed taught to me personally by my Tenshin Shinyo-ryu instructor at Yokohama several years before I joined the Kodokan. The Tsukkomijime can also be executed from underneath your opponent with your legs encircling his body or even from the side. According to the author, it is also possible to apply this method from a Kuzure-Kesagatame or Broken Scarf Hold stance, in which case he tells you to hitch your *left* leg over your opponent's *left side* neck to intensify the power of your joint hand grip on your opponent's throat (Fig. 36).

Fig. 36

KATAHAJIME
(SINGLE WING LOCK)

You apply this necklock from behind your opponent who is seated with his legs spread out. Your left knee is on the mat. Alternatively this method is sometimes demonstrated with the assailant's right knee on the mat. Your right hand is wound round your opponent's throat from over his right back shoulder to grip his left side lapel with the thumb inside, while your left hand with fingers and thumb aligned is passed from under his left back armpit across his back neck to grip your own right wrist from the inner side in an overlapping hold. Then as you pull strongly to the right with your right hand gripping your opponent's left lapel you thrust hard with your left hand grasping your own right wrist and simultaneously tip your opponent in the direction of his right knee. These combined movements should suffice to choke him effectively (Fig. 37).

Fig. 37

GYAKUJIJIME
(REVERSE CROSS LOCK)

In the main the approach to this necklock resembles that of the Katajujijime already described, but the method of gripping your opponent's collar is different. Having secured the astride position on your opponent's torso with your left hand you grip deeply his left collar in the reverse or Gyaku hold which means that your fingers are inside the collar and your thumb is outside with the thumb edge of the wrist digging into the carotid artery. With your right hand you take a similarly deep hold of your opponent's right collar. Both your wrists are bent inwards, and you impart a slight pulling and lifting feeling to his neck as with your body overlapping him you spread both elbows and pull powerfully with both hands to effect the strangulation (Fig. 38).

Fig. 38

When you take up the astride or equestrian position on your opponent's torso your knees and feet on either side on the mat help appreciably to control his freedom of action. And again, as in the case of the Katajujijime, if your adversary is on the stout side, then to obviate the risk of your being capsized you should raise one knee but use both feet to restrain his freedom of movement.

It sometimes happens that in his struggles to escape from this painful necklock your opponent will contrive to twist and overturn your body to one side. In that case you should encircle his torso with your legs from underneath and with your double hand grip draw his neck towards you and so strangle him.

Moreover, you can sometimes enhance the efficacy of the Gyakujujijime by voluntarily throwing yourself to one side of your opponent after confirming your hold, but in that case you must be careful to fall to the side of the elbow of your uppermost arm, e.g. if your right hand and arm are crossed over your left wrist and forearm, then you should fall to your own right side, since it is surely obvious that if you throw yourself to the other side you will automatically weaken instead of strengthening your stranglehold. If your left hand is crossed over your right wrist and forearm, then you should throw yourself to your own left side. For the rest it is optional which of your hands and arms are uppermost.

SODEGURUMA
(SLEEVE WHEEL)

This very effective necklock is executed in a standing position from behind a seated opponent. Your left hand is passed from over his right back shoulder to seize his left side collar in the Gyaku or reverse grip, i.e. fingers inside and thumb outside the collar. Your right hand is then passed across your left forearm and over your opponent's left shoulder to gain a normal grip of the slack of his jacket in the region of his left shoulder. Having confirmed this crossed arm hold you retreat a pace and simultaneously pull your opponent slightly backwards, then pull and lift with your left hand, pull strongly to your right with your right hand and so strangle him. In contradistinction to the Gyakujujijime your target in the Sodeguruma is your adversary's windpipe and not his carotid artery (Fig. 39).

Fig. 39

Choking With Thrust Of Right Hand:
It is assumed that you are lying on your back and that your opponent is either on all-fours or in a sitting posture slightly over you and prepared to resist. Take hold of his left front lapel (with your right hand) in the reverse grip already explained, while with both legs you thwart his efforts to apply a

hold-down. Should his neck and throat be exposed at this juncture, then using your left wrist push powerfully from below upwards against his throat while spreading your elbows, and with your right hand, which has relinquished its preliminary hold of your opponent's left front lapel you hug his back neck from the left side. Your right wrist should make contact with your left wrist from underneath. Then concurrently with a thrusting movement you pass your right leg over your opponent's left shoulder so that from beyond the under part of the knee-joint from his rear neck it extends to his right shoulder-blade or thereabouts. Now while powerfully stretching your leg you thrust more and more with your right hand and with your left pull and press so as to choke your opponent (Fig. 40).

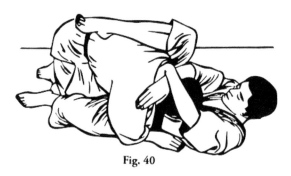

Fig. 40

The foregoing should apparently be regarded as a sketch in broad outline of the basic movements in this particular method of Shimewaza. But the author goes on to elaborate and supplement it with additional emphasis on the action of arms and legs which suggests the possibility of introducing certain variants calculated to increase the efficacy of this necklock. The points covered relate to:

Use of your right hand:

(1) This hand hugs your opponent's back neck.

(2) The same hand may clutch your own left sleeve. In special cases you may simultaneously with your right hand grip both your opponent's lapels.

Use of feet and legs:

(1) It is permissible to encircle your opponent's trunk with your legs.

(2) Both feet may be used with a thrusting tightening movement against your opponent's front waist. In that case care should be taken to prevent your opponent from escaping by twisting his body to the left.

(3) Insert both feet from your opponent's waist to his thighs and from his inner thighs spread them so as to immobilize his movements in that direction.

Method Of Choking By Hooking With Left Leg:

In this method your opponent is lying on his back and you spread yourself over him from his right side. With your left hand you grip his left side collar, your thumb inside. Your right hand is thrust underneath his left armpit so that you are in approximate control of his torso. Now you should bear heavily forward with the upper part of your body and then pass your left leg over your opponent's face so that the bend of your knee-joint presses firmly against him from his left side neck almost to his back neck. Now impart as much forward pressure as possible to your left front waist and hips while with the tension of your left hand on your opponent's left side collar you choke him into submission (Fig. 41).

Fig. 41

It is sometimes possible to convert this form of assault into a left armlock (Hidariudegatame) or alternatively into a reverse cross chokelock (Gyakujujijime) against an unwary opponent. Such tactics are technically styled Kenyoho or combination methods.

Method Of Choking By Gripping Left Ankle:

This necklock is without a doubt one of the most drastic and hitherto most unorthodox in the entire Shimewaza repertoire. In the execution of it you take hold of your opponent's rear collar from the direction of his left side lapel in the familiar Gyaku or reverse grip. Then with both legs you encircle his torso. It may then happen that your opponent will be tempted to resort to Osaekomi or a hold-down and to that end his right hand may be thrust forward from the direction of your left inner thigh.

You are, of course, at this stage lying on your back with your opponent bending over you. Now pass your left leg behind your opponent's head from his right side neck, the rear side of your knee-joint pressing firmly against the back of his neck. With your right hand grip your own left ankle from above and strongly tighten the frontal and downward tension of that hand while simultaneously imparting a sensation of stretching to your left thigh. With your left hand reverse grip on your opponent's left back collar pull powerfully to your left and in this manner the coordination between your left leg pressure against the back of his neck and the leftward traction of your left hand may very well choke him into submission.

It should not be necessary to explain that this impressive necklock can, according to circumstances, be equally well applied by substituting your right leg for your left and your right hand for your left. In that case, of course, you must pass your right leg over your opponent's left shoulder and use your left hand instead of your right to seize your ankle, and grip his right back collar with your right hand in the reverse hold against his neck. And from this point you must synchronize the downward traction of your left hand ankle hold with a sustained pull to your right with your reverse hand grip on your opponent's right back collar (Fig. 42).

Fig. 42

Doubtless considerable practice will be called for before you may hope to master the knack of this necklock. Correct synchronization and sequence of the relevant movements are indispensable to its success.

Method Of Choking By Concentrating Weight Of Body On Left Wrist:

An opening for recourse to this method may occur when you have been attempting a Kuzure-Kamishihogatame or Broken Locking of the Upper Four Quarters against your opponent from his right side and he is trying to capsize you to his left side. In that case grip his left side collar with your left hand, your thumb inside (the normal hold) and your wrist in close contact with his throat. Pass your right hand from under your opponent's right armpit so as to grip his back collar in the reverse hold. Suddenly draw and lift with your hands so that his throat and neck are exposed, and bring his back neck to rest on the top of your left thigh. Draw and tighten strongly with your right hand while your left hand with tension applies a throttling pressure to his windpipe and you bring the weight of your body to bear upon your left wrist until he is forced to submit to avert unconsciousness.

According to circumstances it may be more convenient to reverse the order of grip and to use your left instead of your right hand for the hold on your opponent's back collar. Again while lying on your stomach or on all-fours you could not place your opponent's back neck on your left thigh; instead you might then go for a Left Rear Scarf Hold or Hidari-Ushiro Kesagatame (Fig. 43).

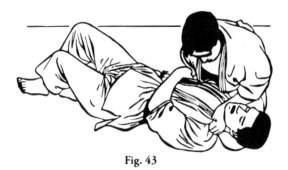

Fig. 43

Method Of Choking From Direction Of Head:

It is assumed that your opponent is in a half-sitting or half-lying position or on all-fours. Bending over him pass your left hand round his right side neck so as to grip from underneath his left side collar with the fingers inside, otherwise the reverse or Gyaku hold. Be careful to establish the closest possible contact between your left wrist and your opponent's windpipe. Pass your right hand under his left back armpit so as to grip his right front collar also with the four fingers inside—the reverse hold. Your opponent's back head should be held against your chest and emerge from under your left armpit. Both your legs should be stretched to the rear so as to bring your weight to bear heavily down upon your opponent. Both your hands are used to apply the maximum tension to left and right respectively, combined with the pressure of your chest so as to choke your opponent into submission. Additional efficacy can be given to this method by using your superimposed weight to bend your victim's encircled neck and by lifting his trunk (Fig. 44).

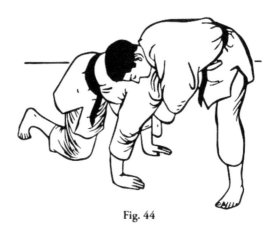

Fig. 44

Method Of Choking By Winding Arm Round Left Collar:
This method may be applied to an opponent who is on all-fours perhaps on the point of rising in front of you. With your right hand passed over the back of his left side neck and under his throat grip his jacket a little lower than his left front collar, your thumb inside (the normal hold); pull strongly with that hand from his left front to the right, your hand and forearm being so to speak coiled round his throat and neck. Plant the inner side of your right knee so that it is in close contact with your opponent from his left front neck to his back neck. Combine the pressure of your right knee with the maximum tension of your right hand against your opponent's throat and neck until submission is extorted to avoid suffocation. Your left hand plays a

very minor role in this method, and can be placed against your opponent's right Waist (Fig. 45).

Fig. 45

Method Of Choking From Underneath By Gripping Your Own Cuff:

This method may be enlisted as an effective counter to your opponent's attempted Kamishihogatame or Kuzure-Kamishihogatame (Locking of the Upper Four Quarters or Broken Locking of the Upper Four Quarters) respectively. Pass your left hand from over your opponent's throat and neck and seize his right side collar with the four fingers inside and so that your left wrist is held tightly against his neck and throat. Pass your right hand over his right side neck to his back neck and take hold of your own left cuff. Then as you stretch the front of your torso raise your left hand and draw it nearer with your right hand clutching your left cuff. In this way your opponent's windpipe is crushed from front and rear and his breathing cut off. According to circumstances the order of this grip can be reversed, i.e. your left hand may be used to grasp your right hand cuff (Fig. 46).

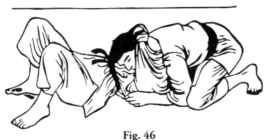

Fig. 46

Method Of Choking From Underneath:

This method is also a retort to an attempted Kamishihogatame or Kuzure-Kamishihogatame respectively. Pass your left hand from under your opponent's throat to grasp his right side collar with the thumb inside—the normal hold—and with your right hand similarly take hold of his left side collar. Utilizing the weight of your body pull his neck to the left side while you bring your body to the right, bend both legs, inhale deeply, stretch your torso and use both hands to choke your opponent. In some cases you can advantageously encircle your opponent's neck with both your legs to strengthen the strangulation (Fig. 47).

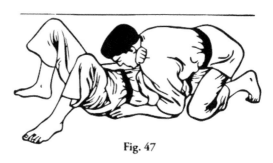

Fig. 47

Method Of Choking From Underneath Opponent With Hand And Leg:

This method too can sometimes be effectively applied to frustrate your opponent's attempted Kamishihogatame, when of course you are lying on your back and your opponent is attacking from behind your head. Pass your right hand under his throat so as to seize his left side lapel in the reverse hold, palm uppermost and fingers inside and at the same time push in the direction of your legs. Bend your left leg so that the thigh touches his head. Raise your right leg and pass it over your opponent's right side neck to his back neck and exert downward pressure with the under part of the knee-joint. Concurrently hold your right forearm firmly against your opponent's throat while with your left hand you grasp your right ankle from above or alternatively, if more convenient, your foot near the toes. In this way from the front and back your opponent's windpipe is crushed with the downward traction on your right leg and the pull to your right with your right hand gripping your opponent's left side lapel (Fig. 48).

The principle of this method with use of the leg is analogous to that exemplified in the method of choking illustrated in Fig. 42, save that in the latter case you use your left leg against an opponent bending over you from your front as you lie on your back, and your left hand is used to grasp his left back collar in the reverse grip.

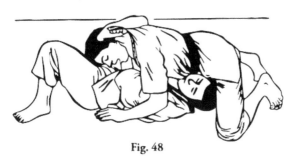

Fig. 48

Method Of Choking By Capsizing Self:

In this case it is assumed that you and your opponent are engaged in Tachiwaza or standing position. With your left hand grasp your opponent's right side collar in the normal hold, palm downward and thumb inside, and with your right hand seize his left side collar in a similar grip. Then as you draw both hands nearer to each other raise as it were your opponent from below and hanging on to him twist your body to your right or left till he is behind you and let yourself fall on to your back to the mat. This manoeuvre will automatically cause the crossing of your wrists as you retain your initial hold on both his side collars. From this supine position hook your opponent's back neck from the direction of his right side neck with your right back knee-joint and bring your left ankle into juxtaposition with that leg.

Apply your right fist closely to your opponent's throat and neck with a drawing lifting action as that hand grips his left side collar and simultaneously co-ordinate this movement with the choking tension of your left hand gripping his right side collar. The combined pressure of your legs and hands, if effectively exerted, may suffice to choke your victim into submission (Fig. 49).

Fig. 49

It may be advisable to suggest that recourse to this method in a real fight in contradistinction to a friendly Judo bout governed by fixed rules might conceivably expose you to an attack by your opponent against a highly vulnerable portion of your anatomy, seeing that his hands would still be free! Therefore for the success of this method in deadly earnest much would depend upon the disconcerting effect of your initial double hand grip on your adversary's throat from the original standing posture, swiftly followed by your turning movement and drop to the mat.

Method Of Choking By Encircling Opponent's Neck With Both Thighs:

An opening for recourse to this necklock may offer itself when your opponent is an all-fours and you are behind him. In that case it is essential for the success of your attack that you should first of all get astride his back horse-riding fashion from the rear. Then you pass your right hand from over his right back neck and under his throat so as to grip his left side collar, and similarly pass your left hand from over his left back neck and under his throat so as to grip his right front collar. From this point swiftly substitute for your position astride your opponent's back one in which his neck is firmly held between your inner thighs. Taking care not to relax this hold, twist your body slightly to one side and roll on to your back, still retaining your initial hand grip on your opponent's left side collar and right front collar. This movement should bring your opponent also on to his back with his head and neck between your thighs as you lie behind him. Now combine a drawing choking action of both hands with the scissor-like pressure of your thighs against both sides of his neck, thus compelling him to submit to avert strangulation (Fig. 50).

Fig. 50

Method Of Choking By Utilizing Your Armpit:

It is assumed that your opponent is in a half-sitting, half-kneeling posture on the mat. Swiftly take up your position kneeling to the right side of his head facing him. Pass your left hand round from his right side neck and under his throat so as to grasp his left side collar with your four fingers inside (the reverse hold palm uppermost) and with your right hand grasp your opponent's middle back belt or left rear side belt so that his head protrudes from under the hind side of your right armpit. Maintain the maximum contact between your right armpit and the joint of your opponent's right side neck. Then as you draw your left hand gripping your opponent's left side collar strongly to your left lean heavily against his right side neck so that under this crushing joint pressure and tension his respiration is cut off and he is forced to submit (Fig. 51).

Fig. 51

D-Style Choking Method:

For this method it is presupposed that your opponent is on his back and that you are contemplating an attack from behind his head. Your right leg passes round your opponent's left side neck across his chest until it links up with his right armpit, while your left leg passes under his back so that the bend of the knee-joint comes in contact with your right ankle. Now raise your right knee somewhat, pass your right hand across from the left of your opponent's upturned throat to grip his right side lapel from inside your right thigh. Your left hand may be simply thrust under your opponent's left armpit to strengthen your control of his freedom of movement, and to immobilize his left arm. Exert both your legs to squeeze your opponent's trunk and synchronize this action with the maximum leftward traction of your right hand gripping his right side lapel. This combined action may suffice to reduce your opponent to submission (Fig. 52).

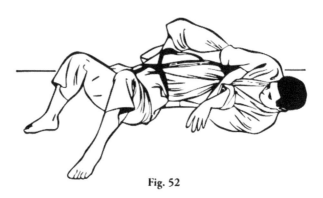

Fig. 52

E-Style Choking Method:

Remember that the basic relative positions for an attack in this style are as follows: Your opponent is lying on his back and you are also lying behind him preferably on your left side. Your right leg is superimposed upon your opponent's right forearm. Your left leg is thrust under your opponent's back right armpit so that his right arm is crushed between both your legs. Your left hand plays a more or less auxiliary role as it passes under his left back armpit to restrict his freedom of movement and the use of his left arm. Pass your right hand from under your opponent's right side neck across his throat and seize his left side collar with the thumb inside. Now draw yourself up and protrude your chest and with the rightward traction of your right hand choke your opponent into submission (Fig. 53).

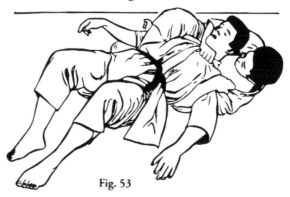

Fig. 53

CHAPTER VII
EXPOSITION OF TRIANGULAR CHOKELOCKS OR SANKAKUJIME

MAE-SANKAKUJIME
(FRONTAL TRIANGULAR CHOKELOCK)

You encircle your opponent's torso with both legs and pull him down. Should he pass his right hand between your thighs, with your left hand you take hold of his left side collar and effect contact between the underside of your left knee-joint and his right side back neck. Further the part below your knee-joint is bent to the right at a right-angle over the back of his neck. Your right thigh crosses his left upper arm and is linked with the back of your left ankle which passes under it approximately at the bend of your right knee-joint to form what the author calls the triangle. Your right ankle is lowered. Your left hand, presumably withdrawn from your opponent's left side collar, seizes his left wrist.

The illustration shows the assailant grasping his opponent's left wrist with both hands. Pulling strongly on it you twist your waist to the left. Both your legs and thighs tightly constrict your opponent's neck from either side. A stretching sensation is imparted to your front waist and in this way perhaps you may control your opponent's respiration with the Mae-Sankakujime (Fig. 54).

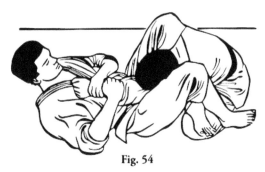

Fig. 54

In case this method proves inadequate, then while you are constricting both your legs against your opponent's neck, spread the palms of both hands against the back of his head and bend it forward so as to intensify the efficacy of the strangulation. Again, if while you are applying the hold your opponent falls on his back, still maintaining control with both your legs get on top of him, draw in your knees to a squatting posture, bend the upper part of your body to the front so that you are virtually on your stomach beyond his head, and endeavour to consummate the strangulation from this position. It is again emphasized that you must ever be on the alert to pass from one method to a variant or Henka, e.g. from a Sankakujime to a Gyaku, and by way of illustration the author cites the following six examples:

A. If in attempting to escape your Sankakujime your opponent begins to get up but falls to his left side, you should hitch your right leg over his right side neck and essay a Jumonjigatame.

B. If in attempting to escape your Sankakujime your opponent begins to stand up, you should seize his (left) wrist with both hands, both your legs encircling him, protrude your front waist, draw strongly on his wrist and gain control of his left elbow-joint.

C. Your Sankakujime may be relatively effective, but if inadvertently your opponent lets his left arm dangle then with both hands grip his left wrist, push and lift it to the right side and effect control of his left elbow-joint.

D. If while applying the Sankakujime your opponent has his left arm bent at the elbow, seize it with your left hand, hitch the fingers in your right thigh, stretch and lift his left elbow and so control the elbow-joint.

E. Again if your opponent chances to hold his left arm bent at the elbow, then with your right hand grip his left wrist, bring his left elbow in contact with your right inner thigh, with your right hand twist his left wrist to the right and so control his elbow-joint.

F. If your opponent in trying to escape your Sankakujime falls on his back, then while still maintaining the strangulation pressure, lie on your stomach and go for an Udegatame or an Udekujiki wherewith to control his left elbow-joint.

URA-SANKAKUJIME
(REAR TRIANGULAR CHOKELOCK)

If your opponent is lying on his back you move round to his head and left shoulder. Your left hand passes under his left back armpit to grip your own left front or right front collar. Your right leg is hitched over his left side neck to his chest and right armpit and your left leg passes under his back so that the underside of the knee-joint is linked with your right front ankle. Thus concurrently with the restraint imposed upon his bodily movement you interrupt his respiration (Fig. 55).

It may happen that when you are maneuvering for an opening to apply the Ura-Sankakujime your opponent fearing a Gyaku will take hold of your front belt with his left hand and tug strongly on it. You should then retort by controlling his hand with your belt as described in Chapter III (Fig. 13-A).

If unfortunately your opponent manages to extricate his left hand you may be able to effect transition to the customary Kuzure-Kamishihogatame or Broken Locking of the Upper Four Quarters. On the other hand, if you are confident in your ability to press your Ura-Sankakujime to a successful issue, then while confining his neck with both your legs, as illustrated in Fig. 55, stretch them and endeavour to cut off his respiration.

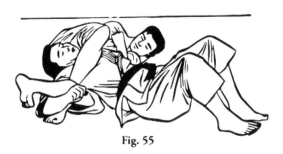

Fig. 55

Or again, as with the Ura-Sankaku you restrict his freedom of action you impart a slight opening sensation to your right knee; you pass your right hand across his throat and grip his right side collar with the thumb inside. Stretch both legs while applying the strangulation, pull powerfully with your right hand on his right side collar to control his respiration. If you still fail to extort submission then relinquish your right leg hold and instantly hitch the back thigh from your opponent's left side neck to his chest and as you stretch it pull strongly with your right hand on his right side collar to consummate the chokelock.

Four basic methods of transition from the Ura-Sankakujime to Gyaku are described as follows: First, if your opponent defending himself against an apprehended Gyaku tightly seizes your front belt, with your right hand grip his left wrist from above, and passing your left hand under his left back armpit take hold of your own right wrist from above so as to turn his hand, as it were, inside out; then swiftly and powerfully wrench it off in the direction of his right armpit and clamp it between your left shoulder and left neck, in this manner creating a Henka or variant for the application of the Udegatame.

Secondly, bring your opponent's wrenched off left wrist in the direction of your left shoulder, then using your left thigh as fulcrum raise it, then press down your opponent's wrist and secure control of his elbow-joint.

Thirdly, if when you are effecting control by means of the Ura-Sankaku your opponent seizes your front belt with his left hand, turns to the right and creates a gap at his left back armpit, thrust your right hand deeply from his left back armpit and grip his left wrist, apply your left hand to your right fist, twist and raise your opponent's left wrist in the direction of his rear right shoulder somewhat on the principle of the Catch Hammerlock to control his elbow-joint.

Fourthly, when in the course of the Ura-Sankaku your opponent extricates his head or neck, then constrict both your thighs and let them gently slide and curve from his (left) upper arm to his elbow-joint or exchange your right for your left leg hitched to your opponent's right upper arm; with the sole of your left foot press and stretch his right wrist and thus control his elbow-joint. In the foregoing manner, employing the Ura-Sankaku as a basis, you should ever be on the alert to ring the changes on Osaekomiwaza, Kansetsuwaza or Gyaku and the more orthodox Shimewaza. From the standpoint of a genuine tussle these methods are replete with validity and interest and call for unremitting study on the part of the Judo neophyte.

USHIRO-SANKAKUJIME
(BACK TRIANGULAR CHOKELOCK)

For the application of this method your opponent should be either on all-fours or on his stomach and you attack at the back but apparently from the right side and facing in the same direction. Your right hand is passed from his right back neck across his throat to grip his left side collar, and your left arm enfolds his left upper arm from his left back armpit. Clamping his torso in this way you fall either to one side or to your direct rear bringing your opponent over on to his back as you lie behind him. Now your right leg is passed from his right back across his throat bent at a left right-angle and the under curve of your left knee-joint passes over the back of your right ankle from his left back shoulder with which the edge of your toes establishes contact. Both your knees and thighs are brought into action to constrict your opponent's throat and windpipe until he is choked into submission (Fig. 56).

Fig. 56

If this Ushiro-Sankakujime misses fire, then raise the upper part of your body, grip your opponent's right or left wrist and pull strongly on it so that it is pinned between your left shoulder and your left side neck, and you apply the Udegatame instead. Or alternatively you may seize his left wrist and pushing it to the left side control his elbow-joint. Here again is exemplified the efficacy of transition from one type of technique to another in conformity with the principle of Henka or variant.

GYAKU-SANKAKUJIME
(GYAKU TRIANGULAR CHOKELOCK)

You have fallen on your back and your opponent is trying to apply a Yokoshihogatame or Lateral Locking of the Four Quarters from the right side. You bend both legs; with your left hand you push his left side neck strongly in the direction of your feet. You raise your left leg, and from your opponent's left side neck to his back neck bring the under curve of the left knee-joint in contact at right-angles, and passing your right leg from his right back armpit hitch the under curve of the knee-joint to the back of your left ankle. Lower your ankles, and bringing both your thighs as near as possible control your opponent's respiration. This method is unfortunately not illustrated.

If while you are applying the Gyaku-Sankakujime your opponent's right hand touches your right shoulder, you may promptly go for an Udegatame. Also while applying a Gyaku you may manage to overturn your opponent to your left side when you should get on top of him, bring your knees as near as possible, and in this seated position draw yourself up, stick out your chest, and essay a chokelock. Again, if this effort fails, perhaps an Osaekomi, e.g. the Tate-Shihogatame or Lengthwise Locking of the Four Quarters may prove more successful.

In a word, always be ready to ring the changes on all three divisions of Katamewaza or Groundwork.

CHAPTER VIII
INTRODUCTION TO KANSETSUWAZA

THE Kansetsuwaza, literally "Ioint Technique", often called in English "Dislocation Methods" or the "Art of twisting and bending the Joints", but more tersely in Japanese simply "Gyaku", is undoubtedly one of the most important branches of the art of Judo. It is a particularly effective means of achieving control over an opponent's body by unnaturally stretching, bending, twisting and inflicting unbearable pain on any joint so attacked. Thanks to the subtlety and finesse of Kansetsuwaza, the Judoka well versed therein can, without himself using much strength, defeat a much more powerful but less skilled opponent. And in this context the tyro will do well to remember that coupled with the zest and interest inherent in Kansetsuwaza is the element of danger, so that once he realizes that there is no avenue of escape left to him he should lose no time in giving the signal of defeat by lightly tapping his opponent's body twice with his free hand or the mat with his feet. This signal indicates that his opponent is the victor.

Inasmuch as the ruthless recourse to Kansetsuwaza may involve injury to sinews and muscles and fracture and dislocation to bones and joints, in orthodox Judo schools or Dojo employment of these methods is restricted in contest to sufficiently skilled Yudansha or Black Belts. Even so, the possibility of accident arising from a too sudden or violent application of Gyaku cannot be excluded, so that these methods ought never to be used in the absence of Yudansha thoroughly versed in the art of Katsu or resuscitation and bone-setting.

Moreover, mindful of the grave physical inconvenience that would inevitably ensue from injury to a Judoka's leg, the rules of both practice and contest generally confine the application of Kansetsu holds to the elbow-joint, injury to which, although undoubtedly unpleasant, would not be quite so disastrous as lameness resulting from a leg fracture. This exception, not mentioned by Oda in his introduction to the Kansetsuwaza section of his book, is the Ashigarami or Entangled Leglock, familiar to all seasoned Judoka, Japanese or Western, a detailed description of which is included in Oda's work. It is directed against your supine opponent's knee, usually the left, which could easily be dislocated if the lock were pressed *a outrance* and your opponent failed to give the signal of submission in good time. And although it may not be easy to estimate to a nicety the various gradations of danger involved in attacks against the leg, I personally am at a loss to appreciate the logic of permitting the Ashigarami while at the same time forbidding the Ashihishigi or Leg Crush, the objective of which is not your opponent's knee but the tibia, fibula and the sensitive fleshy under part of the leg immediately above the ankle. I cannot see that there is much to choose in the domain of disablement between dislocation of the knee and fracture of the tibia or fibula. No such solicitude for the safety of contestants was manifested in feudal days in Japan when few methods were barred in Jujutsu shobu or contests. In this respect, however, times have changed and if, apart from the Ashigarami, leg holds are now demonstrated at all, then it is only in Katame-no-Kata.

Those responsible for the administration of Judo in Japan are rightly anxious that the primary aim of the art as a high-class sport and system of physical and mental training based upon an ethical concept should never be lost sight of, and although it would be sheer affectation to deny that within the limits indicated above Oda's own book furnishes clear evidence of a much wider latitude than would have been permitted some years ago, the embargo hitherto imposed upon unrestricted attacks against an opponent's leg has not been lifted.

In the exercise of Kansetsuwaza, as in all other Judo techniques, you must strive to gain full control over your opponent's body. If you misapply any particular Kansetsu method you are likely to lose contact with his body and thus miss the chance of victory. Therefore be ever on the alert to seize every opportunity. At the same time never overlook the fact that responsibility for not seriously injuring your opponent rests with you.

Kansetsuwaza can be applied alike from the standing position in Tachiwaza, against an opponent on all-fours or on his stomach, when you are on your back or he is on his; from the side and from the rear.

The Judoka conversant with all three branches of Katamewaza, viz. Osaekomiwaza, Shimewaza and Kansetsuwaza, even though less skilled in Tachiwaza, might conceivably in a rough and tumble fight to a finish emerge the victor against an opponent skilled in Tachiwaza but his inferior in Katamewaza. True, against an adversary wholly ignorant of Judo the Tachiwaza expert would surely prove the victor in the wake of a heavy throw on hard ground, but the Katamewaza expert would, of course, know how to breakfall and could thus discount the Tachiwaza expert's superiority in his own particular domain.

The one logical conclusion emerging from all these considerations must be that the zealous Judoka cannot possibly afford to neglect any single section of this great art.

CHAPTER IX
EXPOSITION OF KANSETSUWAZA

UDEGARAMI
(ENTANGLED ARMLOCK)

THE first method to be explained is the Udegarami (Entangled Armlock). This method, if pressed to a finish, can easily dislocate the victim's shoulder and elbow-joint. Like most other Judo technique it can be applied from either the right or left side of a supine opponent and I shall try to describe both these methods.

As you approach your opponent kneeling from his right side he may try to fend you off by seizing your right side collar with his outstretched left hand. In that case with your left hand, back uppermost and directed towards yourself, grip his outstretched left wrist, fingers overlapping and thumb underneath. Push your hand to the front so that the captured wrist is parallel with your opponent's left shoulder and in a position about five or six inches above the mat. Next pass your right arm from approximately under your opponent's left armpit or upper arm, back of hand uppermost, to grasp your own left wrist from above. Then bear down heavily upon your opponent's thorax, prize up your right arm from under your opponent's left arm, so that his left shoulder and left wrist are pressed against the mat. When your opponent's left wrist is immobilized both your knee-caps should be on the mat, but your left knee-cap should touch his right shoulder and your right knee-cap his right side abdomen. Your left elbow from the vicinity of his upper left shoulder is held on the mat. These combined movements should suffice to complete the Gyaku against your opponent's left shoulder and elbow-joint (Fig. 57).

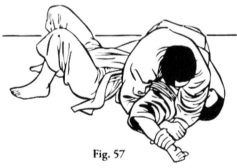

Fig. 57

When in the case of a left side approach you are prizing up your opponent's right arm, his right wrist gripped with your left hand must be held firmly against the mat. The chance to apply this lock from your opponent's left side may occur if he raises his right hand and stretches it perhaps to grasp your collar. Grip his right wrist with your left hand, keep your right knee on the mat, lower the upper part of your body to the front, thrust your right hand under your opponent's right upper arm and grip your own left wrist. Prize up your right arm together with your right shoulder. With both hands press your opponent's right arm to the back downwards to enforce a decision. This method is termed the Hantai-Udegarami or Reverse Arm Entanglement.

It, too, can be executed from your opponent's right side against his left arm as in the case of the orthodox Udegarami. But your left hand is first passed from under his left back armpit and your right hand from over his abdomen firmly grasps his left wrist. Then thrusting deeply with your left hand passed from under his left back armpit, palm uppermost, you strongly grip your own right wrist or forearm. Concurrently with the prizing up of your opponent's left shoulder, as you lift your own, you press your own right wrist downwards with your left hand gripping it from above. These combined movements expose your opponent's left elbow-joint to the risk of dislocation and his left shoulder to painful strain. It will also be seen from comparison of the Hantai-Udegarami with the Udegarami that in the former method your opponent's left arm is nearly straight or only slightly bent outwards, whereas in the latter method his left arm is held quite differently, bent at the elbow to facilitate effective application of the lock (Fig. 58).

Fig. 58

UDEHISHIGI-JUJIGATAME
(CROSS ARMLOCK)

This highly effective armlock is usually initiated from the astride position on your opponent's body and as in virtually every Judo method it can be executed from both his flanks. Your choice of direction would necessarily be determined by your supine opponent's action in exposing his right or left arm to your attack.

If, for example, you are astride your opponent and fearing, say, your intention to apply a necklock he stretches out his right arm to push you off, you would then naturally attack that arm from his right side and conversely should he expose his left arm in the same way, you would then direct your attack from his left side. So much is, as Sherlock Holmes would have said, elementary. Our author's description applies to a left flank attack.

Assuming that your opponent has raised his left hand, instantly seize his wrist with both your hands, your thumbs on the inside and your fingers naturally overlapping. Maintaining this grip throw yourself to your opponent's left flank and simultaneously pass your right leg over his throat till it reaches his right shoulder. Your left knee is raised with your shin held against his left side abdomen. This disposition of your legs is designed to establish control over your opponent's body and so prevent him from getting up. His captured left arm is then clamped between your thighs and for the success of the lock it is essential that the arm should be held with the elbow-joint undermost and pinned into your left or right groin. You should couple the uplift of your waist, lower abdomen and buttocks with the sustained downward traction of your opponent's arm with your dual hand grip. As a rule you hold your opponent's wrist and forearm with your right hand above your left hand which means that the overlapping fingers of your right hand are turned to your left and the fingers of your left hand held below your right hand are turned to your right (Fig. 59).

Fig. 59

The Udehishigi-Jujigatame can also be executed from a standing position. Assuming that in this case you contemplate an attack against your opponent's right arm, you should with your right hand seize his right front collar in the reverse or Gyaku grip and with your left hand take hold of his right outer sleeve. Apply your right foot to his lower abdomen and transfer your double hand grip to his right hand which you pull strongly towards you. Twist your body to the left and let yourself fall to the mat, and to ensure the success of this method it is necessary that the impetus of your fall should bring your opponent to a kneeling position on the mat. Bend your left leg and apply the shin to your opponent's right armpit. Your right leg must now be passed over his left shoulder and across his back neck until the foot is hitched to your left calf or thereabouts. Your inner right knee is pressed powerfully to the left against your opponent's left side head and your left knee to the right against his captured arm so that the Gyaku is effected against the elbow-joint.

Yet another effective method can sometimes be applied against your supine opponent from a position at the left side of his head. If his left arm happens to be held over his chest perhaps gripping his right collar in anticipation of an attempted necklock, you pass your right hand under that arm and take hold of your own left collar with the same hand, while your left hand seizes his back belt. He may then make efforts to escape from a possible immobilization hold. Suddenly pass your right leg across his throat as you pull his captured left hand and arm with both hands—your left hand having been transferred from his back belt. Then fall backwards in much the same way as in the original method described and control your opponent's left elbow-joint between your thighs.

UDEHISHIGI-UDEGATAME
(ARMLOCK)

Your opponent is lying on his back and you move round to his right side to make your attack. You may conveniently have your right knee raised and the left one on the mat or alternatively you may be kneeling. Should your opponent chance to raise his left arm towards your right side neck and shoulder, establish contact between his chest region and your right shin from the knee-cap to the ankle and trap his left wrist between your right side neck and right shoulder in such a way that your right hand with outstretched fingers is placed palm downwards upon your opponent's upturned arm slightly above the elbow-joint and nearer your shoulder, with your left hand also with spread fingers superimposed upon your right hand. Then with both hands you press against your opponent's arm as though in the direction of your abdominal region, twist it somewhat to your right so that the elbow-joint is exposed to the risk of fracture unless your opponent submits in good time (Fig. 60).

Fig. 60

UDEHISHIGI-HIZAGATAME
(KNEE ARMLOCK)

You are engaged with your opponent in Tachiwaza and are holding each other in the normal manner. Plant the sole of your right foot in his left groin and push firmly with that foot; simultaneously trap his right wrist in your left armpit as you fall to the mat on your back. Then the sole of your left foot is placed upon your opponent's right back shoulder while you adjust your recumbent position so that you are lying with your right shoulder undermost. The inner side of your left knee-joint presses heavily against the upturned elbow-joint of your opponent's outstretched arm, the wrist of which is pinned in your left armpit. You protrude your front waist, raise your left side chest, bend the upper part of your body backwards, and in this way effectively control his right elbow-joint.

As in most Judo techniques so with the Udehishigi-Hizagatame variants of hand and leg movements are permissible, their utilization being necessarily dependent on the skill and judgment of the assailant. For example, according to circumstances, instead of pinning your prone opponent's right wrist in your left armpit you may find it more convenient to hold it between your left leg and your left side waist and chest. Or your left elbow may be brought into play to contain his right wrist. Normally your right hand retains its hold on your opponent's left collar which you had taken in Tachiwaza, but its withdrawal need not seriously jeopardize the prosecution of this lock. Instead of planting your left foot on your opponent's right back shoulder you may lightly apply it to his left inner knee. Or the back of the foot may be thrust into his right armpit (Fig. 61).

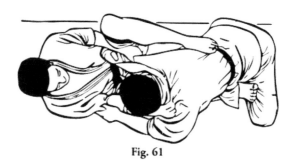

Fig. 61

ASHIGARAMI
(LEG ENTANGLEMENT)

Again you are engaged in Tachiwaza with your opponent and are using the normal holds. Plant the sole of your left foot against your opponent's right inner thigh and push strongly with that foot simultaneously falling on your back to the mat. Now twine your right leg round his left leg from underneath and over it so that the sole of your foot is thrust into his left inner thigh. Your body is switched to your left. You let go your left hand hold on your opponent's right sleeve and together with your right hand grip his left side collar. Pull strongly and couple this movement with the thrusting action of your right foot which is pushed against your opponent's left inner thigh. The effect of these combined movements is to twist his left knee-joint to a degree threatening fracture unless he surrenders in time (Fig. 62).

Fig. 62

The Ashigarami can be equally well applied to your opponent's right leg by simple reversal and readjustment of the relevant hand and leg movements. Thus the sole of your right foot must then be planted against your opponent's left inner thigh from the standing position and your left leg wound round his right leg as you fall to the mat, while your double hand grip is transferred to his right side instead of his left side collar. My own first introduction to the Ashigarami occurred very many years ago when I was privileged to take part in a specially organized demonstration of Jujutsu at the Yokohama Kagacho police station before the late Prince Henry of Prussia who was visiting the port with the German Far Eastern squadron of which he was admiral. I had been paired with the Japanese instructor and greatly to my youthful chagrin it was not long before I was forced to submit to this particular lock of which I had until then been ignorant.

HANTAI-UDEKUJIKI
(REVERSE ARM DISLOCATION OR WRENCH)
AND UDEKUJIKI (ARM DISLOCATION)

I expect that most of my readers are familiar with the Udekujiki applied from the standing position usually from your opponent's right side against his right arm. Briefly in the Udekujiki you turn to your opponent's right rear flank and face in the same direction. With your right hand you grasp his right wrist, back of your hand uppermost, taking care that his palm is uppermost and, of course, his elbow underneath. You hold his right upper arm under your left armpit. Your left forearm is passed under your opponent's right arm so as to link up with your right inner sleeve or lapel. The thumb edge of your wrist and forearm should press upwards against his captured arm. You press down his right wrist and impart upward leverage to your left arm against his right elbow the joint of which is thus threatened with fracture.

Fig. 63

The Hantai-Udekujiki is however applied to a supine opponent. Lying on top of him as though in the act of applying the Tate-Shihogatame or Lengthwise Locking of the Four Quarters you contrive to immobilize his right arm between your left shoulder and side neck. With your left hand you grasp his right wrist. Your right hand is then passed from over the outer bend of his right arm underneath his forearm so as to take hold of your own left wrist. Now press down your opponent's right wrist with your left hand and simultaneously stretch, tighten and raise your right elbow so that his right elbow-joint is placed in jeopardy (Figs. 63 and 64).

Fig. 64

MESHI-TORU-GYAKU
(ARRESTING REVERSE LOCK)

Assuming that your opponent is lying on his stomach you approach him from the direction of his head, first with your left knee on the mat and your right leg bent. Your right hand is passed from your opponent's left chest through his armpit to his back. Now as you make as if to move your body to the left you thrust strongly with your right hand and change your position on the mat by kneeling on your right knee and bending your left leg. Stretch and tighten your right elbow so as to convey the impression that you plan to turn your opponent over on to his back.

This manoeuvre may tempt him to fumble somewhat with his left hand in an effort to clutch part of your clothing. If so swiftly bring your left hand into play and firmly grip his left wrist twisting and raising it in the direction of his right shoulder. This hold bears a strong family resemblance to the hammerlock familiar to all Catch wrestlers (Fig. 65).

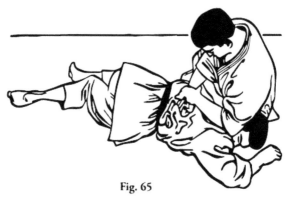

Fig. 65

In an effective variant it is assumed that your opponent may with his left hand grip and pull strongly your front belt when you should pass your left hand through his left back armpit and with your right hand grasp his left wrist. Then with your left hand take hold of your own right wrist and with this double hold twist and pull his left wrist up and over to his back in hammerlock fashion. Unless your opponent is hankering after a dislocated elbow-joint and an injured shoulder he will be well advised to surrender.

No. 1. Lock Applied To Opponent's Right Arm From Broken Scarf Hold
Position:

You are seated at your prostrate opponent's right side facing him as though planning to apply the Kuzure-Kesagatame or Broken Scarf Hold and have already pinned his right upper arm under your left armpit. Your left wrist is thrust from under his right back armpit and your right hand is brought into contact with your opponent's right front shoulder against which it must be firmly pushed. Grip your own right wrist with your left hand already passed under your opponent's right back armpit, bear down heavily in the direction of his right wrist, twist and prise his right elbow-joint upward from left to right and coordinate this action with maximum pressure of your right palm against the point of your opponent's right shoulder. Through this combined movement both the right elbow-joint and right shoulder of your opponent are in danger of dislocation unless he surrenders in time. Other optional alternative holds with your left hand in lieu of the above-mentioned clasping of your own right wrist are:

(1) on your opponent's left lapel with your four fingers inside, i.e. the reverse or Gyaku grip;

(2) on your opponent's left lapel with your thumb inside—the normal grip; and

(3) on both your opponent's front lapels with similar grips (Fig. 66).

Fig. 66

No. 2. Lock Applied To Opponent's Right Arm From Broken Scarf Hold Position:

As in the previous method you are attacking your prostrate opponent from his right side facing him as though planning to apply the Broken Scarf Hold. Now if your opponent should pull out his right arm from under your left armpit firmly grip his right wrist with your left hand and using your right thigh as fulcrum press your opponent's right arm, elbow undermost, against it. Help the movement by raising your right thigh and simultaneously push heavily downwards with your left hand against his wrist. To ensure the complete efficacy of this method it is not sufficient to apply downward pressure only with your left hand grasping your opponent's right wrist; you must reinforce the movement by bringing to bear above that hand the inside of your left knee-joint (Fig. 67).

Fig. 67

No. 3. Lock Applied To Opponent's Right Arm From Broken Scarf Hold Position:

In much the same way as in the first two methods already described you are making a feint at applying the Broken Scarf Hold or else the Hongesa (Main Scarf Hold) to your supine opponent. Should he withdraw his right arm from under your left armpit to a bent position seize his right wrist with your left hand, push it in the direction of withdrawal, anchor your right ankle against that wrist, press down the wrist and raise your thigh thus imperiling his elbow-joint. Further, in order to nullify your opponent's efforts to stretch or withdraw his right arm, you can hitch your left knee-joint to your own right ankle and relinquish your left hand hold on your opponent's right wrist, relying solely on your legs to maintain control (Fig. 68).

Fig. 68

No. 4. Lock Applied To Opponent's Left Arm By Enfolding It Under Right Armpit:

Approach as for attack with Broken Scarf Hold. If your opponent tries to withdraw his right arm and to bring his left hand from your front chest towards your forearm (?right), contrive to wedge his left wrist in the region of your right thigh and groin; pin his left upper arm firmly under your right armpit; grip his left wrist with your right hand from underneath and similarly with your left hand his left wrist from above. Stretch and lower your right armpit, raise his wrist and imperil the elbow-joint.

The following additional details are added:

Manner of using arms: Hitch your right wrist from the elbow-joint to your opponent's wrist from the left elbow-joint.

Your stance: You have taken up your position for application of the Scarf Hold, with your right leg extended to the front and your left leg trailing behind slightly raised. If you bend forward so that you are almost lying on your stomach then your right leg will tend to be stretched to the rear.

Manner of using leg when confronting opponent in upright position:

(1) Your right foot may be pushed against opponent's right inner thigh.

(2) Your left foot may be used to push against opponent's right inner thigh so as to cause him to fall on his face (Fig. 69).

Fig. 69

No. 5. Lock On Opponent's Right Arm When He Tries To Counter Your Broken Scarf Hold:

If when you seem to be planning to apply the Broken Scarf Hold from your opponent's right side he tries to turn you over to his left side, quickly raise your left front chest and the upper part of your body and shift your stance in the direction of your opponent's head more or less behind and bending over it. You must contrive to bring him over on to his right side. In this position you withdraw your right hand and place it against your opponent's exposed right back armpit and simultaneously trap his right upper arm under your own right armpit while with your front waist you bear down heavily upon his trapped upper arm and grip his extended wrist with your left hand. The palm of your right hand which, an already mentioned, is placed against his right back armpit, may be planted on the mat close to his upper body. This method is not easy to describe without the illustration to which the reader is referred. However, it will be realized that as your opponent is lying on his right side and almost on his stomach with his right arm awkwardly extended to his own right, that arm must be painfully immobilized when bending over his right shoulder from behind with your right arm held against his exposed right armpit and his right upper arm under your own right armpit, you grip his right wrist with your left hand and in this position subject his right elbow-joint to the concurrent and coordinated downward pressure of your front waist and chest and the upward prizing of the captured wrist with your left hand (Fig. 70).

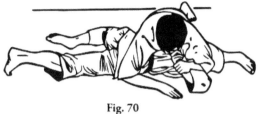

Fig. 70

Gyaku Applied To Opponent's Left Arm From Broken Scarf Hold Position While Hooking Opponent With Left Leg:

The stereotyped approach from your opponent's right side is again pre-supposed. And again he may essay to counter your Broken Scarf Hold by trying to turn you over to his left side and get up. Trap his left arm firmly under your left armpit, holding his wrist with both your hands. Bring your left leg over his chest in such wise that its back hooks the area midway between his left shoulder and left side neck and pushes hard against it. Protrude your left front waist, raise your left armpit, curve your body somewhat backwards and then lower it so that your opponent's left elbow-joint is at your mercy. It may sometimes happen that your opponent will push against your right side neck with his left hand, then stretch his left leg and hook you from underneath in an attempt at counter-action against your contemplated lock. Generally speaking, however, the assailant on top enjoys an advantage, although the stature of the assailant has an appreciable bearing on the issue. In the rather poor illustration to this method the assailant is shown leaning well over his victim's torso with his left leg stretched across his victim's chest and left side neck. Much practice will be needed to get the hang of this difficult lock (Fig. 71).

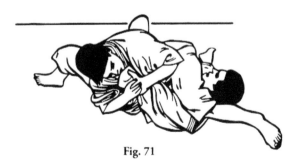

Fig. 71

Gyaku On Opponent's Left Arm From Rear Scarf Hold Position:

You are assumed to be in the apparent act of applying an Ushiro-Kesagatame or Rear Scarf Hold to your opponent with your right side against his left flank as you sit with your back turned to your opponent looking towards his legs. An opportunity to execute this lock may occur if your opponent tries to get up to his left. His left wrist should be snugly held under your left armpit with your left palm pressed against his left elbow. Bring your left leg over your opponent's torso so that it stretches upwards from his right side abdomen to his side chest. Switch the upper part of your body to the left and from this position prostrate yourself forward over his head, simultaneously stretch your left leg, protrude your left front waist, curve the upper part of your body backwards and raise your left armpit under which your opponent's left arm is pinioned. These movements properly executed should suffice to threaten his left elbow-joint with dislocation. In a note about the use of your left leg the author observes that in addition to gripping your opponent's left wrist with your left hand you can advantageously press your left inner knee against it (Fig. 72).

Fig. 72

No. 2. Gyaku Against Opponent's Left Arm From Rear Scarf Hold Position:

You begin from the same posture as before with your right side against your opponent's left flank looking towards his legs. Your left hand is applied to your opponent's left elbow and his left wrist is pinned under your left armpit. Your right leg is stretched obliquely over your opponent's body from the abdominal region to the border of his right side waist with strong pressure. Raise your front waist and lower abdomen. Your right hand gripping the edge of your opponent's right front shoulder prevents him from getting up. Your two bodies are lying face upwards parallel to each other as you fall backwards thereby intensifying the pressure of your left hand against your opponent's left elbow. Alternatively your right foot may be hooked in your opponent's right inner thigh. In this manner control is effected over your opponent's left elbow-joint (Fig. 73).

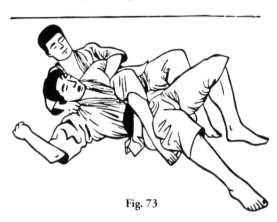

Fig. 73

Gyaku Against Opponent's Right Arm From Locking Of Broken Upper Four Quarters:

You are in a squatting posture behind your supine opponent's head in the act of applying a Locking of the Broken Upper Four Quarters. If your opponent twists his body to the right and from your right front waist and abdomen thrusts it between your left groin and waist, advance your right knee-cap obliquely towards his trunk, grip his right wrist with your left hand and press its inner side downwards so that it is pinned to your right groin; stretch your left leg to the rear, press your right front waist and stomach against the outside of his right arm pushing strongly so that his right elbow-joint is endangered.

In simpler terms, your opponent's right arm is pulled across your right thigh well up against the groin as the weight of your right front waist and stomach bears heavily down upon his right elbow-joint which is thus in danger of fracture. Your opponent's body is turned well over to his right with his right arm immobilized as described above. Your right hand may rest on the mat near your opponent's right side waist. In the original text there has obviously occurred some confusion between left and right—a by no means uncommon error in Judo textbooks and one that is difficult to avoid. Thus

the author speaks about the advance of your left knee-cap and the stretching
of your right leg to your rear although the photographed in this case perfectly
clear—depicts exactly the opposite (Fig. 74).

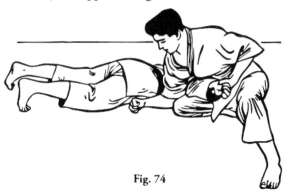

Fig. 74

Gyaku Against Opponent's Left Arm By Trapping It Under Armpit:

As before you are attacking your opponent with the Locking of the Broken
Upper Four Quarters. If he tries to get up to his left see that you capture his
left arm and hold it strongly under your right armpit and that with your left
hand you grip his right side collar with the thumb inside so that you can
frustrate his efforts to rise. Pass your right leg over his chest so that the bend
of the knee-joint presses heavily against his throat while your extended left
foot is brought into contact with his chest and abdomen to control his body.
Constrict both thighs. Fall backwards and simultaneously stretch your
opponent's left arm, raise your front waist, lower your wrist and so threaten
your opponent's elbow-joint. This method may perhaps be regarded as a
variant of the more familiar Udehishigi-Jujigatame or Cross Armlock already
described but one in which
the dynamic of threatened
dislocation proceeds from the
trapping of your victim's left
arm under your right armpit
and not from a hold in which
his arm is held in your crotch
as in the Udehishigi-
Jujigatame (Fig. 75).

Fig. 75

Gyaku Against Opponent's Left Arm From D-Style Position:

It is assumed that you have already effected control over your opponent's body in the D-style explained in Chapter V. Remember, he is lying on his back and from behind his head while lying on your left side you have passed your right leg across his left side neck and throat to his right armpit and your left leg under his back to link up with your right foot.

Fearing Gyaku against his left arm he may take hold of your front belt and pull strongly on it. The author here omits to specify which hand your opponent uses for this purpose but later in the description we learn that it is his left hand. Now with your right hand grip his left wrist firmly while with your left hand previously threaded through his left back armpit you grasp your own right wrist. Now turning towards your opponent's right armpit abruptly and with a concentrated effort pluck his hand from your belt and bring it towards your left side neck so that his arm is sandwiched between your neck and left shoulder. Now both your hands should be applied to his left elbow-joint, and as in the case of the Udegatame by drawing it towards your chest and abdomen and exerting the pressure of your left shoulder you achieve control over it.

In a variant you thrust your right hand though your opponent's left back armpit and clutch the wrist of his left hand grasping your front belt, place your left hand over it, pluck away his hold, twist and raise his wrist towards his upper back and by thus menacing the elbow-joint with dislocation enforce submission (Fig. 76).

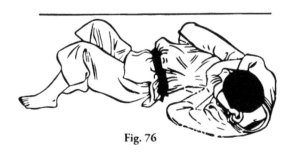

Fig. 76

Gyaku Against Opponent's Right Arm By Holding It Between Both Legs:

Although the author does not say so, we must logically infer from the context that the first moves are made from the standing position or in

Tachiwaza. Fearing your attack your opponent may intersect your arms, take hold of your front or side collar, draw in his chin and drop on all-fours to the mat. In that case move to his right side and neck, thrust your left hand under his left back armpit and seize his right front collar; then pass your right hand from his right side neck, grasp his left side collar and pull him backwards as though for the purpose of applying the Okurierijime or Sliding Collar Lock already described in the Shimewaza section.

Do not forget that the Oda method differs from the erstwhile more customary one applied kneeling from behind a seated opponent in that you are lying underneath your opponent who is stretched out face upwards on top of you. However, in this case you are presumed (from the photograph) to be lying on the mat behind your supine opponent almost athwart his back with your head to his left, and you still retain your hand holds on his neck from that position.

Thrust your left knee and foot under his right armpit so as to stretch his right elbow; if the joint is bent thrust and stretch your right back heel, link your left foot with your right instep, constrict and stretch your inner thighs and with the sole of your left foot press hard against your opponent's right wrist. These combined movements may suffice to control his right elbow-joint. An incidental advantage accruing from this method is that should it fail in its primary purpose you may still find it possible to fall back upon a chokelock, say the Okurierijime, seeing that you have not relinquished your arm holds on his neck. The versatile and resourceful Judoka must be ever on the alert to take advantage of every opening and so to convert failure into success (Fig. 77).

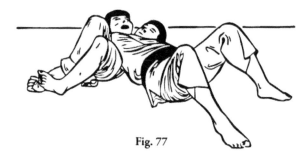

Fig. 77

Gyaku Against Opponent's Right Arm Which Is Grasping Your Side Belt From Your Inner Thigh:

Assume that you are lying on your back and that your opponent passes his right hand from your left inner thigh and grasps your left side belt with it. His left hand clasps your right leg and he is kneeling on the mat or is on his stomach. Now with your right hand grip your opponent's back belt midway and as you pull it raise the upper part of your body and at the same time extend your left foot deeply against his chest from underneath his crouching torso. With your left hand firmly grip his right wrist and bring the instep of your left foot into contact with his left chest from under his right armpit. Tensely thrusting and pushing with your foot turn the upper part of your body somewhat to your left and in this way control his right elbow-joint.

It is also admissible first to grasp your opponent's right wrist with your left hand and afterwards with your right hand take hold of his back belt midway. Again, instead of his belt you may grip his left front collar with your right hand or alternatively use that hand to grasp his right wrist. Or the upper part of your body need not be raised or alternatively it may be raised and somewhat turned to your right instead of your left side (Fig. 78).

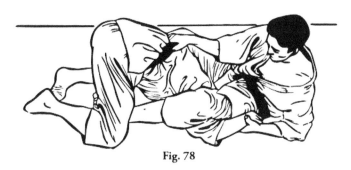

Fig. 78

Gyaku With Your Left Arm Against Opponent's Left Arm Pinned Against Your Thigh:

With your left hand gripping your opponent's left collar fall on to your back and encompass his torso with your legs. Should he take hold of your front collar with his left hand, then with your right leg from below the knee-joint hook him from inside his left upper arm to his back neck and push downwards to the left. Your left arm is held against his arm from elbow to wrist and tightly wedged against your right thigh. Synchronizing the switch to your right with your body with a leftward twist imparted to your opponent's left elbow you may succeed in controlling his elbow-joint. The explanation goes on to say that your right hand may grip your opponent's left wrist or even both your hands may do so (Fig. 79).

Fig. 79

Gyaku Against Opponent's Right Arm With Your Right Knee Held Against His Front Shoulder:

As you lie on your back and assuming that your opponent bending over you chances to bring his right arm close to your left armpit, trap it under that armpit; place your left foot against his right back shoulder; apply the inside of the knee-joint of that leg to the outside of his right elbow-joint; bend your right knee and apply the leg to your opponent's torso from his right chest to his side neck taking care that your knee presses strongly against his right front shoulder.

This movement must be coordinated with the impact of the inside of your left thigh and knee on your opponent's right elbow-joint. The writer suggests that this effective elbow-lock may provide a useful substitute for the orthodox Hiza gatame or Knee Armlock, earlier described, should your opponent try to evade the latter by thrusting forward his right arm (Fig. 80).

Fig. 80

Knee Armlock With Left Leg Over Opponent's Right Shoulder:
You have fallen on your back and have encircled your opponent's torso with your legs and he is on his knees before you. He has passed his right hand from your left inner thigh to grip your left side belt, and his left hand is passed over your right thigh. Now with your left hand grasp his left side collar and with your right hand his left outside sleeve midway and pull strongly on it. Meanwhile your opponent with his right hand holding your left side belt tries to turn your body to your left and to penetrate to that side, whereupon you hook him with your left leg from his right shoulder to his back. Simultaneously you bring up your right knee to your right armpit and apply its inner side to the outside of your opponent's left elbow-joint while with your left leg you exert the utmost pressure against your opponent's right side neck as though trying to force it in the direction of his left side back. Lift your right inner thigh and bring your right knee up towards your front chest in this manner controlling your opponent's left arm and threatening the elbow-joint with fracture (Fig. 81).

Fig. 81

*Gyaku Against Both Your Opponent's Arms With Both Your Legs
Encircling Him:*

As you fall on your back clinging to your opponent you encircle his torso
with your legs. He may then as he bends over you contemplating perhaps a
Jujijime or Cross Necklock grip your front collar with both hands. When
both his arms are thus extended hitch your right leg from your opponent's
left upper arm over his left shoulder from the knee-joint to the ankle, and
your left leg similarly from his right upper arm over his right shoulder so that
both your legs are crossed at the ankles at his back. Both your arms are passed
with linked hands across your opponent's arms extended in their joint hold
on your front collar, although the photograph shows his hands as placed
rather on either side of your neck. If, however, they are both holding your
front collar then your linked hands and arms would be laid upon them nearer
to their wrists. Then as you force them downwards you should raise your
front waist and abdomen, stretch and push downwards both your legs and in
this manner effect control over both your opponent's elbow-joints. It may
happen that your Gyaku proves efficacious against only one of your
opponent's arms instead of both but even so it should suffice for the purpose!
(Fig. 82).

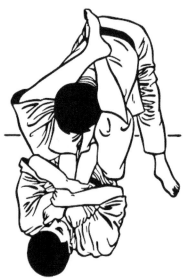

Fig. 82

Gyaku Against Opponent's Elbow-Joint With Both Knees:

You have fallen on your back and with both legs are thwarting your opponent's efforts to penetrate your defences and assail you with Osaekomiwaza or immobilization tactics. Now if with his right hand he grasps your left front collar, pull it strongly towards you, envelop his right upper arm with both legs, and while so doing impart a slight rightward twist to that arm but then bring his right wrist to your left and with the help of your knees pressed powerfully against it control his right elbow-joint (Fig. 83).

Fig. 83

Gyaku Against Opponent's Left Arm By Throwing Him Sideways:

Encircle your opponent's torso with both legs and fall on your back. With your left hand grip his left side collar and pull strongly on it so as to manoeuvre him into a more or less squatting posture between your thighs. If it happens that he passes his right hand from your left inner thigh and with it grasps your left side belt and approaches your right armpit with his left hand, trap that arm under your armpit, apply your right foot to his left inner thigh and place yourself on the *qui vive.*

Your opponent may then with his right hand push away your left foot and try to escape to his left side, whereupon with your left foot you should strike his right side neck so as to cause him to fall sideways while simultaneously with your right foot you press against his left thigh so that from his left side he falls on to his back. Then bring the outer side of your opponent's left elbow-joint over your right thigh and bring your right leg into action on the principle of the Hizagatame or Knee Lock. Push his body with your left foot; use your right thigh as fulcrum; press down his left wrist and so endanger his left elbow-joint (Fig. 84).

Fig. 84

Gyaku Against Opponent's Right Arm As Retort To Shoulder Lock:

The author's description is not so clear as it might be. It is stated that you have been subjected by your opponent to a Katagatame or Shoulder Lock, presumably from your right side and that in order to extricate yourself from it you raise both legs as high as possible, then lower them forcibly and utilize the reaction or recoil in order to bring yourself over towards your left shoulder and so squirm on to your stomach. So much has to be taken for granted. In the next stage your opponent is supposed to be on all-fours and you are on the mat with your back turned to his lowered head. You seize his right wrist from below with your left hand and draw his upper arm under your right armpit. Now grip his right wrist also with your right hand and with your right side chest and right side waist press down heavily upon his outer elbow-joint, at the same time prizing up his wrist with both hands. This combined action may suffice to control your opponent's right elbow-joint (Fig. 85).

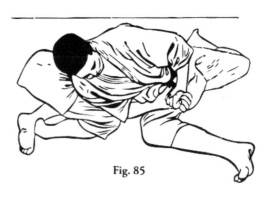

Fig. 85

Gyaku Against Opponent's Outstretched Right Arm:

In this case you and your opponent are standing. With his right hand he may grip your left front collar. If so, then with your left hand you should seize his left front collar, the four fingers inside, and with your right hand his right wrist. Your left shoulder should be thrust forward and your left hand grip on his left front collar tightened with a thrusting action. Stretch your opponent's right arm to the fullest extent so as to control his right elbow. Study of the attached figure will help you to master this particular Gyaku (Fig. 86).

Fig. 86

Gyaku Against Opponent's Left Arm From Equestrian Position:

Your opponent is lying on his back and you are astride his stomach. If he chances to raise his (left) elbow and lower his wrist, then with your right front chest press down upon his left forearm and with your right hand grip his left wrist. Your left hand is hitched to his left forearm. Pull and turn his left wrist in a left outward direction thus imperilling his left elbow-joint (Fig. 87).

Fig. 87

Gyaku Against Opponent's Left Arm From Direction Of Head:

Your opponent is lying on his back and you are attacking from behind his head. An opening for attempting this Gyaku may occur if he exposes his left arm with the inner side upward and bent. Wedge his left wrist between your left shoulder and left side neck. Place your right hand against your opponent's left upper arm from above his left armpit and similarly your left hand against his upper arm from the outside. Crushing force against your opponent's left elbow-joint is achieved through the downward pressure of your left shoulder reinforced by the weight of your body behind it. Both your hands holding his upper arm from either side pull strongly and in this way you may succeed in controlling his left elbow-joint (Fig. 88).

Fig. 88

Gyaku Against Opponent's Right Arm From Astride His Stomach:

You are astride your opponent's stomach as he lies on his back on the mat, but in such wise that your right knee is on the mat and your left knee raised. Should your opponent stretch his right arm, seize his right wrist with both hands. Apply the inner side of your left knee-joint to his right outer elbow and push it inwards. Push his right wrist to the left and so control his right elbow-joint (Fig. 89).

Fig. 89

Gyaku Against Opponent's Left Elbow With Use Of Right Leg:
You have encircled your opponent's torso with both legs and have fallen
on your back. Your opponent is in a half sitting posture or on all-fours. He
has taken hold of your right or left front collar with his left hand. With your
left hand you grip his left wrist from the inside, and with your right hand his
left outer sleeve midway. Your left foot is thrust against his right thigh.

Concurrently using both hands you pull downwards in the direction of
your left armpit. Your body is inclined in the direction of your right back
corner. Your opponent has fallen forward. Pass your right leg from your
opponent's left upper arm to his back neck and use this leg to push him
downwards to your left. At this stage your hand holds are slightly changed.
Thus the outspread palm of your left hand is placed against your thigh (?left)
and with your right hand you grip your opponent's left wrist instead of his
outer sleeve. You tighten your hold so as to raise his left elbow when the joint
under the impact of your right thigh is exposed to fracture failing timely
surrender. When applying this type of Gyaku against your opponent's elbow-
joint you must make sure that the elbow-joint is uppermost, otherwise the
lock cannot succeed (Fig. 90).

Fig. 90

Gyaku With Opponent's Left Wrist Under Your Left Armpit:
You have encircled your opponent's torso with both legs and have fallen
on your back. In contemplation of an Osaekomi he may with his right hand
thrusting from your left inner thigh have veered to the left side. In that case

with both hands clutch either his left inner sleeve or cuff and abruptly and with maximum force pull that arm in the direction of your left armpit. Concurrently hitch the underside of your left knee-joint over your opponent's right side neck with the feet opposite his back armpit. His left wrist should now be hugged in your left armpit.

Your front waist is raised and bending backwards you control your opponent's left elbow-joint. Your right leg is passed along his head and face with the inside knee-joint hitched and stretched against his left side neck. The figure shows the assailant's feet linked together (Fig. 91).

Fig. 91

Gyaku Against Opponent's Left Arm Held In Left Armpit:

Although the author fails to say so the context and illustration indicate that you make your attack from behind your opponent as you both lie on your backs. You encircle his torso with both legs. With your left hand you grasp his left collar and with your right hand his outer sleeve and drag him backwards as you fall behind him. With both hands you pull him strongly in the direction of your left armpit. Now with your right hand you seize his back belt and continuing, from his right back armpit you grasp his front collar with the four fingers inside. Your left hand passes from his left rear shoulder to his back so that his left upper arm is hugged firmly in your left armpit. You establish contact between your opponent's left rear flank and the upper part of your body. Pull and stretch with your right hand. Draw your left armpit to the rear. Your left foot should be placed as far as possible in the direction of your opponent's right armpit. Now with your legs you encircle his chest.

A sensation of somewhat bending back is imparted to the upper part of your body and in this manner you should control your opponent's left elbow-joint. Your right hand may also be passed from your opponent's right back shoulder across his throat to take hold of his left front collar (Fig. 92).

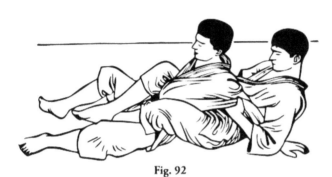

Fig. 92

Gyaku By Hitching Left Leg In Opponent's Right Arm And Raising Body:
At first you are seemingly maneuvering for a Jujigatame or a Hizagatame but judging from the photograph you must be attacking your opponent as he lies on his stomach or on all-fours although the author does not mention this important detail. The assailant is shown seated on the mat on his opponent's right side and facing in the same direction. You immobilize his right arm, which is pushed from your left waist towards your right thigh, by slipping your left leg under his right shoulder and linking the inside of your right knee-joint with the instep of your left foot, triangular-wise. You raise the upper part of your body. With your right hand you grasp your opponent's back collar and with your left hand your opponent's jacket in the region of his left back neck. You bring your loins somewhat to your right flank and simultaneously as you exert pressure with your legs you bend the upper part of your body to the front to effect control of his right elbow-joint. The illustration scarcely coincides with the letterpress description since the assailant is depicted with his right hand on the mat (Fig. 93).

Fig. 93

Gyaku Effected By Inserting Opponent's Right Arm In Right Back Armpit:

This method is implemented from a standing position. Your opponent takes hold of your left front collar with his right hand whereupon with your left hand you grasp his right cuff. You draw back your left foot and coordinate this action with a pull on your opponent's arm with your left hand causing him to stagger forward somewhat.

At this point you advance your right foot to the front of his right foot and simultaneously pass your right arm round his right arm from above so that it is hugged in your right armpit with the elbow uppermost. Your right wrist is wedged against your opponent's front chest. Continue to pull with your left hand holding your opponent's sleeve and let your body lean heavily on your opponent's right arm. These combined movements may suffice to effect control over his right elbow-joint (Fig. 94).

Fig. 94

Gyaku Against Opponent's Right Arm From Holding Cuff:

You are engaged in the standing position. Your opponent seizes your left front collar with his right hand whereupon with your left hand you take hold of his right cuff and with your right hand his left front collar. You then plant your right foot in his left groin and as you push strongly with that foot fall on your back. At the same time the sole of your left foot is applied to the right back of your opponent who has pitched forward to his right front corner, and is pushed against it. The inner side of the knee-joint of that leg is brought into contact with your opponent's right elbow-joint (which must be uppermost). Your right hand grips his right wrist. Bring it towards your left flank. Press to the right downwards with your left knee and in this way you will threaten your opponent's elbow-joint with fracture (Fig. 95).

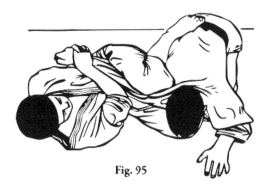

Fig. 95

Gyaku Against Opponent's Right Elbow-Joint Through Hitching Right Leg:

Your opponent is assumed to be in a half-sitting posture. You have fallen on your back. An opportunity for essaying this method may occur if he grasps your front collar with his right hand. Then with both hands you grip his right cuff and as you pull strongly on it you hitch your right leg from over his right arm with the side of the instep held in contact with your opponent's front chest from his right back armpit. You pull more and more with your hands and as you bring him towards your left flank you stretch your right leg and subject his right elbow-joint to pressure threatening dislocation (Fig. 96).

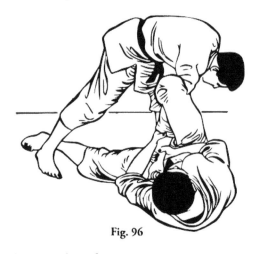

Fig. 96

Gyaku Against Opponent's Right Arm By Wheeling:

Your opponent has from the standing position grasped your left front collar. In your turn with your left hand you take hold of his right front collar, the thumb inside, and with your right hand his right wrist. From this stance you must contrive to dive under his right armpit, still retaining your initial hold, and then fall on your back. Thrusting strongly with your left hand on his right front collar you push his right wrist with your right hand so that his arm is exposed to Gyaku and he, too, falls forward. If you continue this movement *d outrance* he will finally be reduced to extremities and forced to submit (Fig. 97).

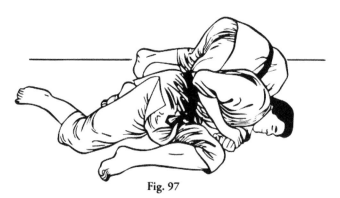

Fig. 97

Gyaku Against Opponent's Right Arm From Left Side Supine Position:

You have fallen to your left side. If your opponent advances his right arm between your thighs you may essay this method. With your left hand you grip his right wrist and with your right arm enfold his upper arm; apply the inner side of your right knee and thigh to the upper arm and as you push strongly down with them use both hands to control his right elbow-joint (Fig. 98).

Fig. 98

Gyaku Against Opponent's Right Arm With Both Legs From Below:

As before you have fallen to the left sideways. Your opponent moves round towards the back in a squatting position. Should inadvertently his right arm chance to be hanging loosely you may attempt this method. With your left hand take hold of his cuff. Raise the back of your left ankle, hitch your right leg from his right forearm and bring the back of that ankle into contact with the rear side of your left knee-joint. Effect as close contact as possible between your thighs, relinquish your left hand hold, stretch both legs, raise your feet, and in this manner control your opponent's right elbow-joint (Fig. 99).

Fig. 99

Gyaku Against Opponent's Right Arm By Twisting And Raising It:

The author leaves one to infer that both you and your opponent are on the ground since he states that you have attempted a Hizagatame against your opponent's right arm and that to escape it he has turned that arm inwards and simultaneously moved to the back. In that case with your left hand you seize his (right) wrist and apply your right hand to his elbow-joint. With your left knee you push downwards the outer side of his right arm and twist and push his wrist in the direction of his left shoulder. If necessary you may grip his right Wrist with both hands. These movements should suffice to control his elbow-joint (Fig. 100).

Fig. 100

Gyaku Against Opponent's Loosely Dangling Arm:

It is here assumed that your opponent is on his stomach and that you have perhaps been contemplating an Okurierijime or similar necklock against him. He has raised his buttocks with both hands on the mat preparatory to getting up. Your right knee-joint is hitched from your opponent's left back shoulder to his side neck and front chest. Your left leg is thrust from his left rear to his chest and abdominal region. Your left hand is linked from his left armpit with his forearm. Your opponent tends to slip downwards from the direction of his raised buttocks until he stops at the point where, as the illustration shows but the author has omitted to mention, you are gripping his left wrist with both hands and not only with your left hand. From your front waist you protrude your lower abdomen (Shitahara), stretch your right leg, tug on his left wrist and in this way effect control over his elbow-joint (Fig. 101).

Fig. 101

Gyaku Against Opponent's Left Arm In D-Style:

You are assumed to be controlling your opponent in the so-called D-style. This implies that he is lying on his back and that you are about to attack him seated from behind. Your right leg is laid across the left side of his neck and over his breast as far as his right armpit. Your left leg is thrust underneath his back until the under curve of the knee-joint links up with your right ankle. Your left hand may be inserted under your opponent's left armpit and freely utilized to help in immobilizing his left arm. Your opponent may with his left hand take hold of your front belt and give warning of his intention to attempt a Gyaku against you. In that case you should with your right hand seize his left wrist and with your left hand hitched from his left back armpit grip his right wrist. Then as you twist his left wrist you should pluck it away from your belt, sandwich it between your left shoulder and left side neck and control his arm with a species of Udegatame or armlock. It is also feasible to place your opponent's plucked off left arm in your abdominal region, grip his wrist with both hands, push it downwards, protrude your stomach and so control his arm (Fig. 102).

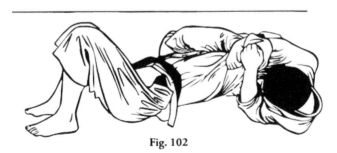

Fig. 102

Another Gyaku Against Opponent's Left Arm In D-Style:

The same preliminaries as in the previous method are postulated. Similarly your opponent may give warning of his plan to apply a Gyaku by gripping your front belt with his left hand, making a gap in his left armpit and seem on the point of switching to the right flank. You should then with your left hand grip his left wrist and thrusting your right hand from under his left back armpit either hitch it to his left wrist or pluck away his left hand from its hold on your front belt, then twist and raise it to his left side and back, thus effecting control over it (Fig. 103).

Fig. 103

Utilizing Opponent's Strength In Applying Gyaku To Right Arm:

You are assumed to be turning sideways or on your stomach. Your opponent moves round to your head with his left knee on the mat and the other one raised. His right arm is inserted into your left armpit and with his left hand he holds your back belt. He may then try to overturn you on to your back by twisting you to the right. In that case you should oppose this manoeuvre by using just a little more strength than he does until you feel that he is tiring when you should seize his right hand with your left hand and pin it under your arm, then utilizing your opponent's strength exerted in his efforts to twist you and with strength exceeding his you turn to the right and get your opponent on to his stomach. With your chest you push down upon his forearm and prize up his wrist thus effecting control over his elbow-joint (Fig. 104).

Fig. 104

Gyaku Against Opponent's Left Arm Held Under Your Right Armpit:

You are assumed to be on all-fours. Your opponent moves round to your head and thrusts his left hand into your right back armpit. Pin that arm under your armpit and slip your head through his left armpit. Lower your right armpit. Lift his wrist and apply Gyaku to his left arm (Fig. 105).

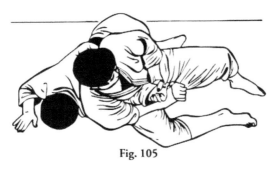

Fig. 105

Another Method:

As before you are on all-fours. Your opponent in a half-sitting posture moves round to your rear. His right hand is thrust from under your right back armpit (sic). As before pin that arm in your armpit, switch your body to your right back corner. Simultaneously withdraw your head to the rear from his right back armpit. With your own right back armpit push down your opponent's right forearm, raise his wrist and apply Gyaku to his elbow. This method is not illustrated which is a pity because the letterpress alone impresses one as not wholly convincing and incomplete. However, as it is the last method explained in this third and final section of Katamewaza, viz. the Kansetsuwaza, I give it for what it may be worth.

GLOSSARY

Ago:	Chin.
Aomuki-ni:	On one's back, e.g. aomuki-ni taoreru (to fall on the back).
Appaku-suru:	To press, to put pressure on, to crush.
Ashi:	Leg, foot, e.g. Ashigarami (Leg Entanglement).
Ashikubi:	Ankle.
Ashi-no-ko:	Instep.
Asai:	Shallow (applying to hold, etc.).
Atama:	Head.
Ataru:	To touch, to be touched by.
Bogyo:	Defence.
Boshi:	Thumb.
Chikara:	Strength.
Chokkaku:	Right-angle.
Chugoshi:	Half-sitting, half-rising posture.
Dembu:	Buttocks.
Do:	Trunk, body.
Eri:	Collar, lapel, e.g. Erijime (Collar or Lapel Choke).
Fufuku-suru:	To lie prostrate.
Fukai, fukaku:	Deep, deeply (applying to hold).
Fukurappagi:	Calf of the leg.
Futo-momo:	Thigh.
Gyaku:	Reverse, e.g. Gyakujujijime (Reverse Cross Lock).
Gyakugeki:	Counter-attack.
Haibu:	Back (human).
Hairikata:	Method of entry to effect immobilization.
Hando:	Recoil, reaction, counter-action.
Hantai:	Reverse, opposite, e.g. Hantai-Udegarami (Reverse Arm Entanglement).
Hara:	Stomach, belly.
Harabai-ni:	On one's stomach.

Hasamu:	To clip, to hold between; usually in Judo applied to encirclement of opponent's torso with legs.
Henka:	Change, variant, mutation.
Hiji:	Elbow.
Hiji-kansetsu:	Elbow-joint.
Heso:	Navel.
Hima:	Space, gap.
Hitai:	Forehead.
Hiza:	Knee, e.g. Hizagatame (Kneelock).
Hizagashira:	Knee-cap.
Ichi:	Position, situation, e.g. Karada-no-ichi (posture of the body).
Inko:	Throat.
Ireru:	To insert (arm, hand, leg, etc.).
Jiku:	Axis, axle.
Jukuren:	Skill.
Kakaeru:	To hold under the arm, to enfold.
Kakato:	Heel.
Kansetsu:	Joint, sinew, e.g. Kansetsuwaza (Dislocation Methods).
Kami:	Top, upper part, e.g. Kamishihogatame (Locking of the Upper Four Quarters).
Kao:	Face.
Karada:	Body.
Karuku:	Lightly.
Kata:	Shoulder, e.g. Katagatame (Shoulder Lock).
Katamewaza:	Overall term for the three divisions of "Groundwork" comprising Osaekomiwaza, Shimewaza and Kansetsuwaza.
Keibu-seimyaku:	Jugular vein.
Kei-domyaku:	Carotid artery.
Kenyoho:	Combination methods.
Kesa:	Scarf, e.g. Kesagatame (Scarf Hold).
Kikan:	Windpipe.
Kobushi:	Fist.
Kogeki:	Attack.

Kokyu:	Breathing, respiration.
Koshi:	Waist, hip, loins.
Kubi:	Neck, e.g. Kubijime (Neck Choke).
Kujiku:	To crush, sprain, dislocate, e.g. Ude-Kujiki (Arm Dislocation).
Kuzure:	Broken, e.g. Kuzure-Kesagatame (Broken Scarf Hold).
Kyobu:	Chest, breast.
Mae:	Front.
Mageru:	To bend, curve, crook, etc.
Mata:	Thigh, groin, crotch.
Migamae:	Attitude, posture. Synonym: Shisei.
Momo:	Thigh.
Mukozune:	Shin.
Mune:	Chest, breast.
Nejiru:	To twist, to wrench.
Newaza:	"Groundwork" (*Vide* Katamewaza).
Nigiru:	To grip, to grasp.
Nuku:	To extricate, to withdraw (arm, hand, leg, etc.).
Obi:	Belt.
Omote:	Front, exterior, outside.
Osaeru:	To stop, check, curb, restrain, e.g. Osaekomiwaza (Immobilization Methods).
Renshu:	Training.
Sankaku:	Triangle, e.g. Sankaku-Osaekomi and Sankaku-jime.
Sei-suru:	To control.
Semeru:	To attack.
Sesshoku:	Contact.
Shikkansetsu:	Knee-joint.
Shimeru:	To choke, to strangle, e.g. Shimewaza (Necklocks).
Shite	Fulcrum.
Shuchu-suru:	To concentrate.
Sode:	Sleeve, e.g. Sodeguruma (Sleeve Wheel).
Sorimi ni naru:	To draw oneself up, throw back one's head, stick out one's chest.

Tate:	Length, e.g. Tate-Shihogatame (Lengthwise Locking of the Four Quarters).
Te:	Hand.
Tekubi:	Wrist.
Teiko:	Resistance, opposition.
Te-no-hira:	Palm. Also Tanagokoro.
Tombogaeri:	Somersault.
Tsukene:	Root, groin.
Tsuma-saki:	Tips of the toes.
Tsuyoi, tsuyoku:	Strong, strongly.
Ude:	Arm, e.g. Udegatame (Armlock).
Undo:	Exercise.
Ura:	Reverse side, back, rear.
Ushiro:	Rear, back, e.g. Ushiro-Kesagatame (Rear Scarf Hold).
Waki-no-shita:	Armpit.
Yoko:	Side, flank, e.g. Yokoshihogatame (Lateral Locking of the Four Quarters).
Yotsubai:	On all-fours.
Yubi:	Finger(s).
Zubon:	Trousers.

Printed in the USA
CPSIA information can be obtained
at www.ICGtesting.com
LVHW020931200724
786057LV00003B/101